WEST
MISSISSIPPI
EDUCATION CONSORTIUM

TEACHER MENTAL HEALTH

DEAR EDUCATOR

We would like to express our heartfelt gratitude to each and every one of you for your support in purchasing our book, "Mental Health Matters: The ABCs of Implementing Emotional Intelligence in Your Classroom." Your dedication to prioritizing the emotional well-being of your students and yourselves is truly commendable, and we are honored that our book has become a part of your valuable resources.

As educators, focusing on your own well-being and mental health is vital, and it directly impacts your ability to create a supportive and nurturing environment for your students. Here are some benefits of why teachers should prioritize their own well-being and mental health:

1. Role Modeling: By prioritizing your own mental well-being, you serve as a positive role model for your students, demonstrating the importance of self-care and emotional resilience.

2. Improved Classroom Environment: When teachers are mentally healthy and emotionally aware, they are better equipped to create a positive classroom environment that fosters empathy, understanding, and effective communication.

3. Stress Management: Prioritizing mental health allows educators to manage stress effectively, leading to higher job satisfaction, improved focus, and better decision-making in the classroom.

4. Better Student Support: Teachers who focus on their own mental well-being are more capable of providing effective emotional support to their students, recognizing and addressing their needs with empathy and understanding.

Remember, taking care of your own well-being is not a selfish act. It is an important part of creating a nurturing and supportive learning environment for your students.

If at any point you feel the need for additional support or resources in promoting mental health and emotional well-being in your classroom, please feel free to visit West Mississippi Education Consortium at www.westmsec.com. Our consortium is dedicated to providing educators with comprehensive resources, training, and support in this important area.

Once again, we extend our deepest appreciation for your commitment to nurturing the emotional intelligence of your students and your dedication to your own well-being. Together, let's continue to build an environment that values mental health and emotional resilience.

With heartfelt thanks,

Dr. Clayton and Rasheda Barksdale

MENTAL HEALTH ALPHABETICAL CONTENTS

THE DECLINE OF EDUCATOR MENTAL HEALTH

Throughout the last several decades, the mental health of educators has undergone a noticeable decline, reflecting the evolving challenges and pressures within the educational landscape. A complex interplay of social, professional, and systemic factors has contributed to this concerning trend. By examining the historical trajectory of teacher mental health, we can gain valuable insights into the evolving stressors that have impacted the well-being of educators.

In the mid-20th century, teaching was often characterized by a sense of professional autonomy and societal respect. However, as time progressed, significant shifts in the educational environment began to take shape. The rise of standardized testing, increased administrative demands, and greater accountability measures imposed on educators created a heightened sense of pressure and scrutiny. Furthermore, budget cuts, understaffing, and expanding administrative responsibilities placed additional strains on teachers' well-being as they strove to meet the diverse and complex needs of their students.

The latter part of the 20th century and the early 21st century witnessed profound societal changes that further impacted educators' mental health. The pervasive influence of technology, social media, and the 24/7 connectivity culture has blurred the boundaries between work and personal life for teachers. The omnipresence of digital communication has led to increased expectations for instantaneous responses, further encroaching on teachers' relaxation and downtime.

Simultaneously, socioeconomic shifts have brought about an increase in the number of students facing various forms of adversity, trauma, and mental health challenges. Teachers have found themselves increasingly burdened with not only academic instruction but also with the emotional and social support of students, often without adequate resources or professional training to address these needs effectively.

Moreover, the COVID-19 pandemic has exacerbated the mental health challenges faced by educators, introducing unprecedented disruptions, anxieties, and adaptive demands. The abrupt shift to remote learning, concerns about personal health and safety, and the emotional toll of supporting students through a period of widespread uncertainty have intensified the strain on teachers' mental well-being.

The decline in teacher mental health over the decades is a multifaceted issue that demands attention and proactive intervention. Understanding the historical context and ongoing changes within the field of education can catalyze efforts to address these challenges. By acknowledging the unique stressors that educators face and implementing targeted interventions, including mental health support, professional development, and systemic reforms, it is possible to work towards restoring and safeguarding the well-being of teachers. Ultimately, prioritizing teacher mental health supports not only the educators themselves but also serves to benefit the students, families, and communities they serve.

The decline of teacher mental health over the decades underscores the need for a comprehensive and evolving approach to address the multifaceted stressors embedded within the educational landscape. By recognizing the historical context that has shaped these challenges, and by implementing targeted support mechanisms and systemic reforms, it is possible to create a nurturing and sustainable environment that prioritizes the mental well-being of educators. This approach is essential for sustaining a healthy, supportive, and effective educational system that benefits both teachers and the students they educate.

THE IMPORTANCE OF EDUCATOR MENTAL HEALTH

The importance of teacher mental health cannot be overstated, as it profoundly impacts educators, students, and the overall educational environment. Teachers play an invaluable role in shaping the future through their guidance, mentorship, and instruction. Prioritization of teacher mental health is vital for fostering a supportive, effective, and inclusive educational ecosystem.

At the heart of the matter is the well-being of the educators themselves. Teachers face multifaceted stressors, including high workloads, emotional labor, and the responsibility of meeting diverse student needs. Compounded by administrative demands and resource limitations, these stressors can have a detrimental impact on teacher mental health. Sustaining a healthy, positive, and supportive work environment is paramount for retaining skilled and dedicated educators and preventing burnout, turnover, and disengagement.

Teacher mental health has a direct correlation to the quality of education and the well-being of students. Educators navigate complex roles that extend beyond academic instruction, often requiring emotional support and guidance for students experiencing adversity or trauma. The mental and emotional well-being of teachers directly influences their capacity to provide this support effectively. Moreover, educators' own mental health profoundly influences their instructional effectiveness, their ability to manage classroom dynamics, and their overall job satisfaction, which in turn resonates with students' academic achievement and emotional development.

Fostering educator well-being is fundamental for creating a nurturing and inclusive learning environment. When teachers are mentally and emotionally supported, they are better equipped to create a positive and empowering atmosphere that encourages student engagement, fosters social-emotional growth, and facilitates academic achievement. Educators who feel supported in their own mental health are better equipped to promote a culture of well-being and resilience within the classroom, leading to positive student outcomes and a sense of overall community wellness within the educational setting.

Addressing teacher mental health is essential for promoting equitable and inclusive educational practices. Teachers serve as role models and influencers, playing a critical role in nurturing a supportive and affirming educational environment, particularly for students from marginalized or vulnerable backgrounds. By prioritizing teacher mental health, educators are better equipped to approach their roles with empathy, understanding, and cultural competence, creating an environment that supports the mental and emotional well-being of all students.

The importance of teacher mental health cannot be overstated. Prioritizing the well-being of educators is fundamental for sustaining a healthy, supportive, and effective educational ecosystem. By investing in teacher mental health through supportive policies, resources, and systemic reforms, we create a foundation for empowered, impactful, and sustainable educational practices that benefit both educators and students. A focus on teacher mental health ultimately underpins the creation of an inclusive, equitable, and culturally responsive educational environment that nurtures the well-being and potential of all individuals within the educational community.

PRIORITIZING MENTAL HEALTH
AS AN EDUCATOR

The well-being of educators is foundational to their effectiveness in the classroom. As teachers navigate the complex, multifaceted challenges of their profession, prioritizing mental well-being is a critical aspect of self-care that not only elevates individual capacity but also deeply enriches the educational experience for both educators and students. Cultivating a positive mental state as an educator, characterized by qualities such as calmness, joy, idealism, patience, organization, genuineness, and self-control, can significantly enhance productivity and, ultimately, contribute to becoming a better teacher.

Calmness is a powerful asset in the educational setting. Teachers who prioritize mental well-being and cultivate a sense of inner peace are better equipped to manage stressful situations and maintain a serene classroom environment. By modeling calmness, teachers impart valuable lessons in emotional regulation and conflict resolution to their students. A composed and centered teacher fosters an environment conducive to learning and can effectively guide students in navigating their own emotions and challenges.

Teachers who approach their profession with joy and enthusiasm often inspire their students, setting the stage for a positive and engaging learning environment. Joyful teachers can infuse a sense of excitement into the classroom, cultivating a love for learning and encouraging students to approach challenges with optimism and curiosity. A positive and joyful teacher energizes and motivates students, creating a space for active participation and meaningful educational experiences.

Idealism is a potent force that fuels the commitment and passion of educators. Teachers who maintain an idealistic view of their role as agents of positive change in the lives of their students are more likely to instill a sense of purpose, hope, and ambition in their students. Idealistic teachers can inspire their students to pursue ambitious goals, contribute to their communities, and effect positive change in the world.

Patience is an indispensable quality for educators, and teachers who prioritize mental health can better demonstrate patience and understanding in their interactions with students. A patient teacher fosters a supportive and inclusive environment that encourages risk-taking, learning from mistakes, and embracing diverse perspectives. Patience also allows teachers to effectively accommodate the varying needs and learning paces of their students, ensuring no learner feels left behind or overlooked.

Organization is an essential ingredient in effective teaching, and mental well-being helps teachers maintain a structured and organized classroom. By fostering clear and consistent routines, procedures, and communication, organized teachers create a sense of predictability and stability for their students, and this enables optimal learning and minimizes disruptions.

Genuineness in the classroom establishes trust and rapport between teachers and students. Teachers who prioritize mental well-being are better able to connect authentically with their students, build stronger relationships, and create a safe and nurturing space for learning. A genuine and empathetic teacher cultivates an environment where students feel valued, respected, and understood, which in turn fosters open communication, collaboration, and confidence in students' academic endeavors.

Self-control is an essential component of effective classroom management and student guidance. By exercising self-control, teachers can model patience, emotional regulation, and thoughtful decision-making. Self-controlled teachers can respond tactfully and effectively to varying student behaviors and situations, fostering an environment conducive to learning and mutual respect.

Prioritizing mental well-being as an educator is foundational to becoming a better teacher. By embodying qualities such as calmness, joy, idealism, patience, organization, genuineness, and self-control, and others that will be discussed in the workbook - teachers can cultivate a positive and empowering learning environment that supports holistic student growth and success. When teachers prioritize mental health, they not only enrich their well-being but also profoundly impact the lives of their students, contributing to a nurturing and effective educational experience.

Mental Health Matters:

The ABCs of Implementing Emotional Intelligence in Your Classroom" is a comprehensive workbook consisting of 26 distinct lessons, each meticulously crafted to fortify the emotional intelligence of educators. By focusing on specific mental health components, this workbook is purposefully designed to enhance the capacity of educators to navigate and respond to the emotional dynamics within the educational environment.

Enjoy!

A

ACTIVE TEACHING

(Exerting influence or producing a change or effect.)

Teachers must be highly active within their classrooms. After teaching their daily objectives and assigning class work, they must walk around the classroom assisting, monitoring, and remediating those students who may not have comprehended the concept of the objectives. Being actively engaged within a classroom will also decrease behavioral problems because teachers will be exerting their authority deterring "would be" discipline problems, thereby creating a positive classroom atmosphere conducive to learning.

Additionally, teachers must be active in their students' lives by attending their extracurricular activities. Many students look forward to seeing their teachers at their games, cheering them on. When I was teaching within the 7-12 public sectors, I enjoyed going to my students' games. I cheered their names, rooted for them, and applauded their efforts. The next day in class, I would pat them on the shoulder and briefly mention how well they performed to the class.

Teachers should avoid that tempting seat behind the teacher's desk but should choose to monitor the class by walking the aisle. Being actively engaged will not only decrease behavioral problems but the teacher will also become more connected with her/his students by dedicating one on one time to them. Active teachers not only have fewer discipline problems and an established connection with more students, but they also manage to burn unwanted calories throughout the day.

MENTAL HEALTH LESSON PLAN

Audience: Administrators, Educators, Central Office Personnel & Staff

Subject: Mental Health

Topic: Active Teaching

LESSON GOALS

○ Provide evidence as to why active teaching is beneficial to youngpeople and educators.

○ Elaborate on how active teaching can positively impact the mental health ofstudent and educators.

○ Provide activities that can bring more active engagement into theclassroom.

CASEL STANDARDS

○ Self-Awareness

NOTES

_____

_____

_____

_____

_____

_____

_____

_____

_____

_____

LESSON OUTLINE

INTRODUCTION

In order to be active as an educator in your district, you must first think about the ways you can engage both your students and yourself in the space. One excellent way of doing this in the classroom is through classroom discussion. Reflection writing can also be a magnificent tool to fully engage everyone. Role playing can bring learning to life, allowing the students to fully absorb their learning. In this lesson you will learn to teach in a way that is very active, both for yourself in the learning process, and for your students to engage with the learning themselves.

STRATEGIES

1. How can classroom discussion facilitate an active teaching model?

A classroom discussion is a dynamic exchange of ideas, opinions, and perspectives among students facilitated by the teacher. It's a collaborative process where students actively engage with each other to explore topics, share insights, and deepen their understanding of the subject matter. During a classroom discussion, students have the opportunity to express their thoughts, ask questions, and respond to their peers, fostering critical thinking skills and promoting active participation. The teacher guides the discussion, ensuring that all voices are heard and encouraging respectful dialogue. Through meaningful discourse, students not only learn from the material being discussed but also from each other, developing communication skills and gaining new perspectives on complex issues.

2. How can reflection writing utilize active teaching methodologies?

Reflection writing is a process through which individuals introspectively explore their thoughts, feelings, and experiences on a particular topic or event. It involves expressing personal insights, reactions, and observations in a structured and thoughtful manner. Reflection writing encourages individuals to critically analyze their experiences, consider the implications of their actions, and identify areas for growth or improvement. This form of writing often involves self-awareness and self-assessment, allowing individuals to deepen their understanding of themselves and their interactions with the world around them. Whether used for academic purposes, professional development, or personal growth, reflection writing provides a valuable opportunity for individuals to engage in meaningful self-exploration and learning.

3. How can role playing be a good example of active teaching?

Role-playing in a classroom setting is an interactive learning activity where students take on specific roles or characters to simulate real-life scenarios or situations. It involves students embodying different perspectives, personalities, or roles related to the topic being studied, allowing them to explore and understand complex concepts from various viewpoints. Through role-playing, students engage in active participation, problem-solving, and decision-making, which helps enhance their communication skills, empathy, and understanding of social dynamics. The teacher typically sets the stage for the role-play scenario, provides guidelines or instructions, and facilitates the activity to ensure productive and meaningful interactions among students. Role-playing encourages creativity, critical thinking, and collaboration, making it an effective tool for experiential learning and skill development in the classroom.

ACTIVITIES

1. Classroom Discussion

Facilitate a discussion about the benefits of active teaching described in the prompt. Encourage educators to share their experiences with teachers who havebeen actively engaged in their learning and extracurricular activities. Discuss howthese interactions have impacted their feelings of connection and support.

Encourage teachers to branch off of one another's ideas, and ask questions to oneanother based on how the conversation is going.

2. Reflection Writing

Have teachers reflect on a time when they felt supported by a teacher outside of the classroom. Perhaps this is when a teacher went to a play, a sports game, or just went the extra mile to show that she cared. Ask them to write about how this experience made them feel and the impact it had on their overall well-being. Also have them elaborate on how this shifted their thoughts around teaching today.

3. Role-Playing

Divide teachers into pairs and assign roles as a teacher and student. Have them act out scenarios where the teacher demonstrates active engagement, such as attending a student's extracurricular event or providing one-on-one support in the classroom. Also have them act out a lack of active engagement, and really encourage exaggeration. It may feel silly - but some teachers really teach this way! Encourage students to discuss how these interactions contribute to a positive learning environment.

REFLECTIONS

1. Classroom Discussion

- How did participating in the classroom discussion enhance yourunderstanding of the topic being discussed?

- Reflect on a moment during the discussion when you encountered adiffering viewpoint. How did this challenge your perspective, and what did you learn from it?

2. **Consider your contributions to the classroom discussion. Were there any instances where you felt particularly engaged or challenged? How did this impact your overall learning experience?**

   ◉ Reflection Writing

   _____

   _____

   _____

   ◉ Think about the reflection writing activity. What thoughts or emotions arose for you as you reflected on your experiences?

   _____

   _____

   _____

   ◉ Reflect on any insights or discoveries you made during the writing process. Did you uncover any new perspectives or gain a deeper understanding of yourself or the topic?

   _____

   _____

   _____

3. **Consider how reflection writing can be applied beyond the classroom. How might this practice benefit you in your personal or professional life?**

   ◉ Role-Playing

   _____

   _____

   _____

- Reflect on your experience participating in the role-playing activity.How did embodying a different role or perspective influence your understanding of the scenario?

- Think about the interactions you had with your classmates during the role-play. Did you encounter any challenges or moments of collaboration? How did these interactions contribute to your learning?

Consider the skills you utilized during the role-playing activity, such as communication, problem-solving, and empathy. How might these skills be transferable to real-life situations outside of the classroom?

Perhaps that is to discuss punctuation, or perhaps that is to add extra detailand use more descriptive language. Whatever you feel is the biggest learning gap in your low, medium and high groups is what you should center your objective around. You may begin working on that."

- Bring everyone back together

- "Thank you all for your engagement with these activities. I hope you learned a lot about how to be actively engaged as a teacher in your students' learning and how to actively monitor, build relationships, and differentiate.There is a lot to learn in all three of these strategies, however I hope this was a good introduction to give you a place to start. Thank you for all the workyou do to educate our youth every day."

B

BENEFICIAL

(Good; promoting or enhancing well-being.)

Teachers should have an inextinguishable desire to promote and enhance the well-being of not only their students but also their colleagues. It should be the goal of every teacher to mold each person in the building into a better person. Educators must stay abreast of the current trends in education and their respective field so their students will journey into the "real world" as functioning young adults having the knowledge to problem solve using modern strategies.

Instructors must adopt the belief that they must continue furthering their education despite the number of years they have been practicing within their field. This will ensure that they are beneficial to their students. Sometimes educators teach from the same set of notes and the unchanged textbook from when they started teaching years ago. This method of teaching is extremely harmful because neither party is being educationally challenged to address the horrid problems in today's society.

Teachers should become members of their content related professional organizations to receive course-related journals and attend annual conferences where current trends and contemporary topics are discussed in detail. For an example, a History teacher should become a member of the National Council for the Social Studies (NCSS). After teachers return from annual workshops they should be allowed to implement the newly learned teaching strategies in their classrooms.

A list of selected professional organizations can be found at the end of this chapter.

MENTAL HEALTH LESSON PLAN

Audience: Administrators, Educators, Central Office Personnel & Staff

Subject: Mental Health

Topic: Beneficial

LESSON GOALS

- ◉ Encourage the exploration and benefits of lifelong learning.
- ◉ Strategize adaptable teaching using data-driven approaches.
- ◉ Identify how to strengthen the educational environment for all stakeholders.

CASEL STANDARDS

- ◉ Responsible Decision Making

LESSON OUTLINE

INTRODUCTION

As effective educators, it is mandatory that we are reflective and adaptive in our craft. The world is constantly evolving, and in order to best serve the young people in front of us, we must commit to a lifetime of learning and accommodating to the newest best practices. We must also be eager to adjust based on our data collection, so that we are teachers teaching students where they are at. We also must acknowledge that how we take care of ourselves impacts how we take care of our students. We need to take ownership of our self care and take it seriously to best serve the people in our schools.

STRATEGIES

Why should educators be lifelong learners?

As educators, we work to foster a love of learning in our students so that they can grow up to be curious, brave, and independent thinkers. How can we encourage a love of learning if we don't practice what we preach? In order to best serve our students, we cannot be stagnant. If we remain stuck in older mindsets or practices, we risk damaging our students with outdated and harmful practices that could negatively impact our students. When we know better, we do better. Therefore, it is up to us to open our eyes to what we do not know.

There are many ways we can commit to being lifelong learners. We can stay up to date with the latest teaching practices, attend professional development regularly, and be active in committees serving different missions for the school community. Whether your jam is social emotional learning, social justice, or cultivating joy, carve space for your passion to grow in the school environment. See if you can join a group that's already established, or get a group together. Many people want to contribute to these aspects of a school community, but don't have an outlet to do so. Begin having the conversations, and start organizing the brainstorming time together.

In addition, it is so powerful when students have teachers to look to who are invested and passionate about interests outside of the classroom. If you are an artist, bring some of your work into the classroom! If you are a yoga teacher, teach your students some poses! If you are a sports fanatic, let your team spirit fly! The more that your students see you as a dynamic and whole person, the more they can see the endless pieces of their identities that they can work to develop. Who knows, your little bit of inspiration might spark a lifetime hobby for them. It's worth the share.

——————————————— *(Now, complete Activity 1.)* ———————————————

How can our teaching be data-driven?

Data-driven teaching is crucial in order to best serve your students at every level. If quizzes and tests are the only way you assess your students' learning, it's time to reacclimate. Many students experience varying levels of test anxiety, and this is not always an accurate indicator to show how much they truly know. A helpful way to collect data is by giving a daily exit ticket, to assess mastery of a skill taught that day. In addition, it can be beneficial to add a question or two to better understand the students' comfortability with the topic. A question such as, "How confident do you feel on this material on a scale of 1-3?" or "Do you feel you could teach someone else this concept?" can help you determine which students are wary of certain topics and which could use some additional support.

With this daily data, you can truly begin to dive into differentiation in the classroom, so you can meet each student where they're at. You can give students additional practice on the topic at hand, give students who need an additional challenge a challenge packet, and begin pulling students for conferences based on how they did on different exit tickets. Students will enjoy and appreciate the more individualized attention, especially if you make it feel like something that is a special treat for students as opposed to a punishment. In this smaller group, students may feel more confident to ask more questions, or feel less afraid to make mistakes.

(Now, complete Activity 2.)

How can we benefit educational spaces for all stakeholders?

Of course, the most important people that benefit from a great teacher are the students. Students are why we have schools in the first place. We want to help young people develop their identities and become the leaders and earthshakers of tomorrow. However, in order to serve our students best, we need to ensure that we are not pouring from an empty cup. Which, although it is against the norm for many teachers, requires us drawing clear boundaries around our work. In addition, it is our responsibility to hold other teachers accountable to taking care of themselves the best that they can.

(Now, complete Activity 3.)

1. Lifelong Learner

Circle the following ways that you continue to advance your learning as an adult.

- ◉ Following the News
- ◉ Reading Nonfiction Books
- ◉ Learning about Diverse Cultures
- ◉ Staying Up to Date with Politics
- ◉ Listening to Podcasts
- ◉ Traveling to New Places
- ◉ Watching Documentaries
- ◉ Following News on Social Media
- ◉ Attending Museums
- ◉ Subscribing to Journals
- ◉ Identify and Fill Gaps in Your Knowledge
- ◉ Reflection on Life Experiences

Count up the number of prompts circled.

If you have 1-4, you are a budding lifelong learner.

If you have 5-8, you are a developing lifelong learner.

If you have 9-12 you are an emerging lifelong learner, but there's always more to learn!

2. Data-Driven

Consider one lesson that you are teaching in the next week. Write the topic here:

In one sentence, write what you would consider "mastery" of this topic.

Now, draft a problem that could illustrate mastery of this topic. Use the space below to brainstorm.

Draft 1-2 questions that ask your students about their confidence with this topic.

3. Beneficial Spaces

List three people who have strong work/life boundaries.

How do you know these people have strong boundaries?

How do they fill their cups?

What's a way that you fill your cup?

Honestly... are you doing this regularly? Or does work always take the front seat?

Make 1 clear and actionable commitment you can make to yourself to do a better job at filling your cup. This commitment starts now.

REFLECTIONS

1. **Lifelong Learner**

   ◉   Are you a budding, developing, or emerging lifelong learner according to the previous activity?

   ◉   Are there any additional lifelong learning ideas you would like to begin exploring?

   ◉   What are some hobbies outside of the classroom that you could bring into the classroom as a way to further connect with students?

◉   How can you continue to develop your personal hobbies?

2. **Data Driven**

◉   Why is it important to understand students' mastery of material (outside of testing contexts?)

◉   Why would you ask students about their comfort level with a topic?

◉   What can you do with the data you collect?

◉   How can collecting data feel manageable as a daily thing to do? How can this get worked into your routine?

3. Beneficial Spaces

◉ What are you looking forward to when it comes to taking better care of yourself?

◉ What are you afraid of?

◉ Who can help remind you of your goal when you begin to doubt your self care priorities?

◉ Who can you help hold accountable to take better care of themselves?

CALM

(Composure; steadiness of mind under stress.)

Teachers should always remain calm; keeping their composure despite a stressful working environment. Teaching is a very stressful occupation if there is poor classroom management, disorganization within the school and overbearing parents. However, teachers should never allow any force outside their home to change their attitude. Oftentimes, students misbehave only to see teachers erupt into a fierce fury of shouts. After students reduce teachers to an animalistic level they feel as though they have control of the class because they know how to alter the teacher's attitude. Teachers should remain composed for the following reasons:

1. Students model adults therefore they need to observe adults correctly managing stressful situations.

2. Once a student realizes that he or she has the ability to frustrate a teacher, that student will make that his or her daily routine. Aggravated teachers are unable to think logically, therefore hurting the educational well-being of other students.

3. Calm, 'together' teachers are able to set the tone of their classroom. Frustrated 'out-of-whack' teachers create a turbulent, out-of-control environment that is not conducive to learning.

4. Lastly, and arguably the most importantly, teachers should remain tranquil because no one should be allowed to steal your joy.

Calm teachers are focused professionals. They understand that stress can be a great motivator at identifying new ways of challenging students but they also know that too much stress at work is damaging to their professional and personal lives. Please stay poised in spite of seen and unforeseen work related challenges.

CASEL Competency: Self-Management

MENTAL HEALTH LESSON PLAN

Audience: Administrators, Educators, Central Office Personnel & Staff

Subject: Mental Health   **Topic:** Calm

LESSON GOALS

Practice attuning to your body through a body scan.

- Brainstorm how to "set the temperature" in your classroom.
- Write your own "grounding moment" to share with your students.

CASEL STANDARDS

- CASEL Competency: Self Management

LESSON OUTLINE

INTRODUCTION

One of the most important things that we can embody as teachers is a sense of calm presence. However, when you think of managing 20 students, teaching, classroom management, answering family emails, and asking students to sign out to go to the bathroom, I'm sure that the first word that comes to mind is not "calm".

However, through some of the techniques we will walk through today, you can use them for yourself and your students to tune into a calmer, more grounded sense of self. In our body scan, you will attune to your physical awareness, and take note of the sensations present in your body. You will consider how you can "set the temperature" in your classroom, so that regardless of what energy steps into your classroom, students can leave feeling more grounded and centered. You will also practice writing a "grounding moment" that is made especially for your students, so you can take these learnings and bring them right with you into your classroom.

STRATEGIES

Body Scan

An important way to stay grounded is by attuning to the physical sensations in your body. Often when we are busy, we can go through life living in our thoughts, worries, and future plans, all while being completely unaware of how it feels to be present in the moment. Through the technique of a body scan, you mindfully notice the sensations in each part of your body. This brings your focus out of your thoughts and cerebral space, and into your sensing body, which can help calm your nervous system and bring you back in touch with the present moment.

A body scan goes from one end of your body to the opposite end. Take your time mindfully noticing the sensations in each part of your body. Body scans are great to do in a quiet space, either seated with your feet planted on the ground, or laying with your back on the ground. Once you practice this, think about how you could bring these concepts into the classroom to teach to your students.

———————————   (Go to Activity 1.)   ———————————

SET THE TEMPERATURE

Another important tool in the classroom is to establish a sense of calm by "Setting the Temperature". When students come into your classroom, they come with a whirlwind of emotions, energies, and anxieties. However, the way that you set up your classroom for the first moments that a student enters, can entirely shift their energy for the day. Say you walk into a classroom after getting in a fight with your friend. You come into the next class, all the lights are fluorescent, everyone is talking and shouting to one another, and your teacher is rushing around making last minute adjustments to her lesson plan. Would this make you feel calm and composed, or only add to the sense of overwhelm? Now, consider if you walked into a classroom where the lights were dim. By standing at the door and letting students know we are only using a whisper voice, the teacher successfully drops the volume from hallway talk to a whisper. There is a fireplace playing on Youtube at the front of the room. There is light meditation music playing. You can smell the lavender essential oil diffuser at the back of the classroom.

The latter is likely the classroom that will create an environment most conducive to learning. Perhaps you'd even exhale and feel a sense of calm by coming into this learning space. By using these techniques, you can "set the temperature" for every class that comes into your room. You have the power to set the tone. You do not have to just be reactive to what comes into your room.

———————————   (Go to Activity 2.)   ———————————

GROUNDING MOMENT

When you notice that there is a lot of energy coming into your classroom, a wonderful teacher strategy to use and model yourself, is taking a moment to ground yourself. By just slowing down, pausing, and reacclimating to a space, students can make wiser choices. We can also make wiser choices as educators and people when we take a moment to pause, take a deep breath, and move from a grounded and centered place.

Grounding moments are simply moments of pause, where students can rest their eyes, tune into their bodies, and take some deep breaths. Take the liberty to make your own grounding moments based on your students and their specific needs. You know best!

ACTIVITIES

BODY SCAN

Either sit comfortably with your back resting against a flat surface, or lay down on the ground. Either close your eyes, or lightly keep them open with your gaze focused on a still spot ahead of you. Beginning at your toes, begin imagining an aura of light that is slowly moving through your body. Any time the light moves toward a body part, take a moment to notice any sensations in that part of your body. Maybe you notice temperature, tingles, numbness, or soreness. Any sensation is okay, just take note of them as we walk through the different parts of your body. Take this exercise as slowly and as mindfully as you can.

First we'll start with your toes, shining the light at the tips of your toes. Then to your toe knuckles, slowly lighting the back of your foot, to your heel. Around your ankle, your lower shin, your lower calves, behind your knees, around your knees, your lower thighs, your upper thighs, your hamstrings, your hip creases, your lower tummy, the space around your ribs, your chest, your neck, your shoulders, your biceps, your triceps, around your elbows, your forearms, your wrists, your knuckles, your fingers, back up to your shoulders, around the base of your neck, the back of your head your ears, your scalp, your face.

Once you've completed the body scan, take a moment to just notice any sensations that are in your body. When you feel ready to do so, you can begin to wiggle your fingers and your toes, and to bat your eyes open and rejoin the current moment.

(Now complete Reflection 1).

SET THE TEMPERATURE

Think of some things that are in your favorite calm "sanctuary". Maybe it's nice music, a lovely scent, or dim lighting. Brainstorm a list below of what pieces of the environment make it a sanctuary for you.

Now think of how you can take these elements of calm and bring them to your classroom. Maybe with some music playing, pulling up a video on YouTube, or simply by turning down the lights. Brainstorm below.

(Now complete Reflection 2.)

GROUNDING MOMENT

Take a moment to notice the chair holding your weight under you. Let your eyes get heavy, and feel free to close them if you would like, or gently gaze at a still object in front of you. Begin to notice your breath. Try not to adjust it in any way, but just notice the inhales and the exhales. If you hear any sounds, just take note of them, and then return to the focus of your breath. If any thoughts come into your head, acknowledge them, and picture them floating away like bubbles. Those things can be thought about later. Take five more rounds of breath, inhaling, and exhaling. Once you have completed your five rounds of breath, you can bat your eyes open and rejoin the class.

REFLECTIONS

BODY SCAN

◉ What were some sensations that you noticed in your body scan?

◉ How did you feel before the body scan? After?

◉ How could you bring this technique into your classroom?

◉ How could you use it more often in your personal life?

1. **Set the Temperature**

   ◉ What do you notice between your sanctuary space compared to your classroom space?

   ◉ How could you make your classroom feel more calm to students?

   ◉ What can you do to prepare your environment for when students enter?

2. **Grounding Moment**

   ◉ When could a grounding moment be helpful in the classroom?

◉ When can a grounding moment be helpful to you throughout the school day?

◉ How can you ensure that students are respectful of one another during their grounding moments?

NOTES

DEDICATED

(Devote -- give entirely to a specific person, activity, or cause)

Being a teacher in today's Age of Accountability is very challenging and often overwhelming. Teachers have to perform a range of tasks including, but not limited to: delivering high powered quality instruction to large classrooms, serving on committees within the school, keeping an accurate database of grades and attendance, preparing lesson plans, calling parents to keep them abreast of their child's grades and behavior, serving as class sponsors and acquiring additional college credits so they can renew their teaching license. The aforementioned duties are only the tip of the iceberg but each requires a lot of time and detail. Nevertheless, every morning devoted teachers wake up and boldly accept and embrace the challenge by trying their best to better every child that they encounter.

Dedicated educators understand that successful teaching requires performing tasks that may not be outlined in the job description. They understand that they have to donate time, money and resources that they may not have. Devoted teachers are the teachers that become flustered when their students don't master objectives not only because they spent hours preparing lessons and tutoring students, but also because they know their students can do better.

One dedicated teacher can awaken the potential of the child that sleeps in class, creating a visionary dreamer. One dedicated teacher, through the unlimited power of prayer and encouragement can guide a child off the path of self-destruction. One dedicated teacher can inspire a room full of children to see something in themselves despite being submerged in repugnant home environments.

MENTAL HEALTH LESSON PLAN

Audience: Administrators, Educators, Central Office Personnel & Staff

Subject: Mental Health

Topic: Dedicated

LESSON GOALS

Consider the educator's current level of dedication to the art of teaching.

- ◉ Remind educators of a dedicated teacher who invested in them.
- ◉ Brainstorm room for further devotion in the classroom.

CASEL STANDARDS

- ◉ Social Awareness

LESSON OUTLINE

INTRODUCTION

When a teacher steps foot in a classroom, they are likely not just doing so for a paycheck. The character of many teachers is built on a commitment to make the future brighter, and to do so with endless responsibilities outside of simply teaching the lessons. Teachers are expected to regularly support families with communication, serve on committees, keep records of learning data, and instruct high quality lessons. Oftentimes, teachers need to take out of their own pockets in order to best serve the young people in front of them, both literally and metaphorically.

Teaching requires a level of empathy and dedication that is far beyond many other career paths. When the many additional roles and responsibilities pile up, it can be easy to feel lost in overwhelm or bogged down by a to do list. However, by grounding ourselves in our devotion, we can remember why we chose the path of teaching. We believe in tomorrow, and we believe the young people in front of us will be the change makers our future needs.

When a teacher is dedicated to their craft, they are holding themselves to a standard that goes far beyond doing their best. They are committed to showing up every day as the most compassionate, resilient, and motivated versions of themselves, so that the young people in front of them see a role model that gives them hope for who they can grow up to be.

Consider the educator's current level of dedication to the art of teaching.

Take a moment to ground yourself and consider, what is the "why" behind your decision to become a teacher? Teaching is not simply a job that pays. It is dynamic, exhausting, and exhilarating. It is considered by many to be an art, a craft, or a devotion. Teaching must mean more to you than something to pay the bills. Consider your level of dedication to this craft, and whether this aligns to your "why". How do you currently live out this mission in your thoughts, actions and words every day so your students can feel your purpose through your teaching?

Maybe a reason you are teaching is to help your students feel known and loved. How are you sharing this with every interaction that you have with them? Maybe you want to empower your students to be leaders of tomorrow. What opportunities are you providing them to become leaders in the classroom? Continue your brainstorming in Activity 1.

————————————— (Now, Complete Activity 1.) —————————————

WHO WAS YOUR DEVOTED TEACHER?

Many teachers have one thing in common. We choose to give back because someone first invested in us. Whether it was your high school math teacher who tutored you or your second grade teacher who went to your soccer games, at some point, someone likely showed you that extra layer of love that made you decide you'd do the same for someone else some day. These outstanding teachers went above and beyond to help you become the person that you are today.

Consider who this person was for you, and move onto Activity 2.

HOW CAN THIS DEDICATION FURTHER DEVELOP IN YOUR PRACTICE?

Teachers in particular are considered lifelong learners. In order to best serve our students, we need to constantly assess and rethink our teaching techniques so we know that our methods will definitely benefit our students long term. Whether this is in how we assess data, the materials we ask students to engage with, or a teaching technique, our craft is always evolving, but only in correlation with how much we are. To continue to best serve our students, we need to commit to this constant growth and redirection because as we know better, we need to commit to doing better.

Consider some ways that you'd like to improve on your teaching practice. When you are ready, move onto Activity 3.

(Now, complete Activity 3.)

REFLECTIONS

Reflection 1

◉   How can your "why" influence your dedication to teaching?

◉   How can you live this out in your teaching every day?

◉   Think of some concrete examples of how you can change your teaching tomorrow to better align with your why, and your devotion.

Reflection 2

◉   What are the qualities that you and this teacher have in common?

◉   How are you different?

⊙ How could you continue to develop your teaching so that your dedication impacts your students positively?

Reflection 3

⊙ Which goal are you most excited to implement?

⊙ How can working toward this goal positively influence your students?

⊙ How can you continue to evolve in your dedication to teaching, and resist getting comfortable in your practices?

EMPATHETIC

(Showing empathy or ready comprehension of others' states.)

Teachers are extremely fortunate to occupy a critical position of encouragement in a child's life. However, some teachers don't embrace the role. When students come to them with excuses, teachers treat them as if they are mind manipulators, trying to work the system. However, this may not be the case in all situations. Let me be frank, there are plenty of students that expect "something for nothing." There are students that want a passing grade even though they have not attempted to master taught objectives. Conversely, there are more students that are truly hurting due to circumstances beyond the confines of their control. It is the teacher's responsibility to offer *empathy, understanding, and guidance* instead of casting a judgmental eye.

Having the ability to offer adamant empathy to understand a student's unfortunate circumstance shows a great deal of maturity on the teacher's behalf. For example, if a student is having difficulty understanding basic math, the teacher should not write the student off as incapable of learning. Rather, the teacher should offer to assist the student and his/her family in locating the proper resources to secure his success. No matter what the impediment: from unplanned pregnancy to misbehaving; from misunderstanding to unmotivated, teachers should be the pillars of understanding, offering stern wise advice and never sacrificing the hurtful truth for *harmful* convenience.

Teachers should be emphatic because they were a student once, looking for someone to lean on just as their students are.

MENTAL HEALTH LESSON PLAN

Audience: Administrators, Educators, Central Office Personnel & Staff   **Subject:** Mental Health   **Topic:** Empathetic

LESSON GOALS

Reflect on personal school experiences and the challenges teachers once faced while being students in the classroom.

- Develop empathy by considering how outside factors can impact a student's behavior in the classroom.
- Practice responding to model student scenarios with empathy.

CASEL STANDARDS

- Relationship Skills

LESSON OUTLINE

INTRODUCTION

When you accept the position to be a teacher, you are accepting a large amount of responsibility beyond the realm of teaching academics. You must also realize that you are becoming one of your student's primary adults in their life, which is not something to take lightly. You impact your students' lives much more than you understand, and your response to their challenges are crucial to their wellbeing.

Students come into our classrooms as complex, dynamic, beautiful human beings. Just like you, they have an entire life outside of the school building. Sometimes, their home lives are challenging. Sometimes, they are sick and fighting through it. Sometimes, you could be the only adult that is truly rooting for them. It is imperative that you do so well, and with extraordinary levels of empathy. In this lesson, we will remind you of your humanness, which we hope you will apply to your understanding of your students each day. Your students are as complex as you are, and the more you remember this truth in your interactions with them, the more positive your impact will be.

STRATEGIES

Reflect on personal school experiences and the challenges educators faced while being learners in the classroom.

We all come with a range of memories from our childhood classrooms. Some are positive and joyful, and some are likely upsetting or anxiety provoking. We spent the majority of our childhood with our teachers, and are likely to remember them distinctly. We will particularly recall the teachers who were cold and harsh. However, the ones that likely influenced us to pursue teaching ourselves, were also the ones who greeted you with warmth, met you with understanding, and checked on you in moments when you needed to be seen.

We will consider our personal memories in the classroom, and think about the variety of teachers that taught us, their teaching styles, and how it impacted us.

——————————— *(Now, complete Activity 1.)* ———————————

Develop empathy by considering how outside factors can impact performance in the classroom.

Next, we are going to consider some of the factors that impact our students every day before they even enter our classroom. As people, we tend to get caught up in our daily to-do's, struggles, and relationships and can forget that everyone else is also wrapped up in theirs. Students face challenges involving special learning needs, stressful home dynamics, and developing hormones to name a few.

In Activity 2, you will read through several examples of challenges students may face throughout their school day.

——————————— *(Complete Activity 2.)* ———————————

Practice responding to model student scenarios.

Lastly, we will consider some ways that we as teachers can respond to our students with empathy. Some days, all a student needs is a passionate, enthusiastic teacher to brighten their mood. On other days, students could use a check in to know that a trusted adult cares about them. Perhaps for students who are more reserved, it can be useful to write them a note as a check in, or to give them a reminder that you care about them and are an open ear if they need to talk to someone.

In Activity 3, you will read some model student scenarios and practice thinking about how you could respond to them with empathy..

(Complete Activity 3.)

ACTIVITIES

1. Take a moment to center yourself. If you feel comfortable doing so, you can close your eyes, or keep a soft gaze. Ground your feet on the earth, and focus on the inhale and the exhale of your breath.

   Now, take a moment to think about yourself as a student. You can think about yourself in some different ages if you'd like, but just take a few moments to ground yourself in your inner child. Consider the feelings that you felt as you walked through your school hallways. Perhaps school was a joyful place for you, or perhaps not. Just take a moment to observe what feelings arise.

   Now imagine yourself entering the classroom of a teacher you remember being particularly disconnected from their students. This teacher never asked you how you were, or checked in on you when you were having a hard day. It seemed that the only reason they were there was to get their paycheck. Think about how the interactions with this teacher affected you. Did it make you feel frustrated? Unseen? Unknown? Consider the thoughts and feelings that come up when you think of being in this classroom.

   Now imagine yourself leaving that classroom, and going to class with your favorite teacher. Think about how this teacher greeted you. Was it with a smile? Was it with a check in, asking you about your weekend or about how your day had been so far? Think about how these interactions with this teacher made you feel. Did it make you feel sure that if something were wrong, that your teacher would be there to support you? Did it help you feel safe in their space? Consider how the energy that this teacher brought to your interactions impacted your mood. Also consider how this impacted your learning in that space.

   Now you can recenter yourself in your body when you are ready. You can open your eyes if you haven't already done so and re-enter the space.

Read through the challenges students could face throughout the school day below. Place a checkmark next to any challenges that you could relate to when you were a student.

- ◉ Friend drama
- ◉ Bad test scores
- ◉ Forgetting your homework
- ◉ Losing a family member
- ◉ Not getting enough sleep
- ◉ Period cramps
- ◉ Worry about school safety
- ◉ Feeling nervous for your upcoming test
- ◉ Being embarrassed by a classmate
- ◉ Nervous for your siblings' doctors appointment
- ◉ Worry if your outfit is not "cool enough"
- ◉ Frustration over not having the glasses you need
- ◉ Parents forgetting to give you your attention medication, making it hard to focus

———————— (Now, complete Reflection 2). ————————

Read the following student scenarios. After each one, brainstorm how you could respond with empathy.

Jeriah came into school this morning upset. She slept through her alarm, and had to walk to school in the rain. Now her hair is wet, her sweatshirt is damp, and she has her head down in class. How could you respond with empathy?

Marco's especially quiet today in class. He's usually the class clown, but today he hasn't said a word. Every paper that you put in front of him, he just doodles on. He went to the bathroom, and it took 7 minutes. How could you respond with empathy?

REFLECTIONS

Reflection 1

◉ What thoughts and feelings came up when you were in the first teacher's room?

◉ What thoughts and feelings came up when you were in the second teacher's room?

◉ How does this inform you to focus on teaching with empathy?

Reflection 2

◉ What feelings came up when you read through these student challenges?

◉ What memories came up when you remember these struggles?

- How can you, as the teacher, support your students with more compassion when they are experiencing these issues?

Reflection 3

- Take a moment to notice what your impulse reaction was in each of these situations. What would this reaction realistically be in the moment?

- Now consider your empathetic response. How could this turn around your student's day?

- Try to come up with a few model case studies on your own, perhaps basing them off a student of yours that you find particularly difficult. How could you approach this student with more empathy the next time they are having a hard day?

FORGIVING

(Inclined or able to forgive and show mercy)

Successful teachers understand the power of being able to forgive the transgressions of a disobedient child, rude coworker, and dogmatic administrator. On any given day a public school building is encumbered with problems. Fortunately, most of the problems encountered are solvable if the parties involved are willing to peacefully settle the situation, _then_ to forgive each other. Teachers and administrators are in admirable, public positions. They cannot hold grudges with students or amongst themselves. Once the situation is successfully resolved teachers must walk away from the incident, not harboring any hatred or ill feelings.   A child will do devious acts for many reasons, but teachers must have the regard to discipline him and move forward; not treating the offender any different from anyone else.

Administrators and teachers should always act professionally especially when there is a degree of hostility between parties. Faculty, for the sake of the children, should try to resolve any conflict or misunderstanding that hinders the growth and success of the institution.

Every institution has its fair share of problems and misunderstandings. Faculty and students must work out the unpleasantness, forgive and move forward!

Forgive. Forget. march Forward.

MENTAL HEALTH LESSON PLAN

Audience: Administrators, Educators, Central Office Personnel & Staff   **Subject:** Mental Health   **Topic:** Forgiving

LESSON GOALS

Identify the negative impacts of holding onto resentment & the benefits of releasing it.

- Establish the impact adult culture can have on young people in school.
- Study strategies to practice forgiveness.

CASEL STANDARDS

- Responsible Decision-Making

LESSON OUTLINE

INTRODUCTION

It is no secret that working in an education space is a difficult task. Daily, an educator is expected to manage the weight of societal inequities impacting their students and their classroom. They must continue to prioritize academic achievement, while simultaneously acknowledging student individuality and their learning accommodations. With all of these high expectations and little support, working in the education system can be extremely frustrating. Sometimes it can become easy to blame co-workers, administrators or superintendents for the seemingly unresolvable issues in your classroom. These challenges can range from boisterous student behavior, to a lack of resources.

However, in order to be the most effective educator that you can be, it is vital that you are able to put aside adult challenges and release harbored resentment in order to best serve the young people in front of you. Although conflict may arise, it is in everyone's best interest to forgive and move forward. In addition, another major challenge of being an educator is managing challenging student behavior. It can be extremely triggering when a student catches on to one of your weak spots, and uses that to their advantage. As manipulative as this may feel, many children develop survival techniques in order to protect themselves. Often, when a student brings extremely challenging behavior into the classroom, this is because they have had to learn how to protect themselves at home. This behavior may seem chaotic and unreasonable for the classroom, however your classroom may be this child's safe space to unlearn these survival tactics. Although it doesn't feel fair, being able to respond to difficult behaviors with understanding and compassion could positively impact that child's life forever.

You establish a sense of safety for that child when they return to school after a difficult previous day and you greet them with a smile and a fresh start. This reliability and trust in an adult is something that could reframe their thought processes and interactions with other people forever. Therefore, it is crucial that we as educators release any negative feelings toward our students so that we are able to show up for them the following day and be the stable, trusting, and safe adults that they need.

STRATEGIES

Identify the negative impacts of holding onto resentment & the benefits of releasing it.

It may feel like the just thing to do when you have been wronged is to hold onto that anger as if your unwillingness to let it go will somehow make the situation right and give you the upper hand. However, this is really not the case. When one chooses to hold a grudge or harbor resentment, this can lead to poor mental health. It seems self-explanatory, but the more that you hang onto anger, the more angry you will feel. The only way to move through these feelings effectively is by accepting the situation and moving on from it.

Often when we hang onto a negative situation it can lead to us ruminating on these feelings. This can then impact our quality of sleep, cause us to feel drained, or lead us to feel more pessimistic. As theory says, the more you focus on something negative, the more negativity will enter your life. However on the flip side of the coin, if you are able to let go and move past a situation that is upsetting, and can think positive thoughts, then you will attract more positivity to your life. Not to mention holding onto negativity can also have a negative impact on your health. Focusing on the negatives can affect proper digestion and effective functioning of your immune system. You can also expect that your social life might suffer a bit, as many people do not choose to surround themselves with people who bring them down. So instead of focusing on the negatives of holding onto resentment, now let's practice flipping and focusing on the positives of practicing forgiveness. In the following activity you will discover the benefits of forgiveness.

_____ (Now, complete Activity 1.) _____

Establish the impact adult culture can have on young people in school.

When thinking about a person's well-being, so much is rooted in the environment that they were raised in. When people are young, their brains, identities and personalities are developing and so much of this has to do with a child's relationship to the adults in their lives. If the primary caregivers for a young person do not respond regularly to the child's needs for reassurance, attention or physical maintenance, this can establish long lasting challenges with attachment as this young person grows into adulthood. Although you do not live at home with your students, you do spend almost as much, if not more, time with these students than their own parents. Therefore, your students pay close attention to whether you can help them meet their needs. Students are highly receptive to the environment that they are in, and will likely pick up on dynamics between adults if they do not seem positive. Whether you realize it or not, you are doing a lot of modeling for your students through how you treat other adults in the building. If you take your positionality and use it to bad talk or spread negative feelings toward another adult in the building, students will learn that this is accepted and repeat that behavior. Therefore, it is really important that educators maintain positive relationships with one another and model that in front of their students so young people can see what healthy relationships look like and begin to form their own.

In the next activity, we are going to reflect on a time that we saw a positive and negative adult relationship, and how these impacted us.

——————————   *(Complete Activity 2.)*   ——————————

Study strategies to practice forgiveness.

Forgiving someone seems like a relatively easy thing to do. However, if we don't know where to start with actually engaging with forgiveness, it is likely that we will really struggle with it. Luckily through the developments in mindfulness and positive psychology, we are able to engage with forgiveness through different lenses that resonate most with the person wishing to forgive. In the following activity, we will look at some different strategies to release anger and resentment toward someone else and to work toward forgiveness.

(Now, complete Activity 3.)

ACTIVITIES

Accentuate the Positive

Read through the following benefits of forgiveness and star the ones that feel most beneficial to you.

- ◉ More mental space
- ◉ Mental clarity
- ◉ Focusing more easily on your work
- ◉ Enjoying cherishing the present moment
- ◉ Future interactions with this person that are positive and nourishing
- ◉ Knowing that you are taking the high road
- ◉ Allowing more space to acknowledge the gratitude you have for this person or situation

(Now, complete Reflection 1.)

How Did Adult Culture Influence You?

Take a moment to think about a time where you witnessed a negative interaction between two adults.

Now, taking a step back and thinking about that situation, what bigger narratives did that illustrate for you and how adults treat one another in the real world?

Now, take a moment to think about a positive relationship that you witnessed when you were younger.

Zooming out, what did this positive relationship teach you about healthy and strong adult relationships?

3. Forgiveness Methods

From the list below, star at least one strategy that you feel might work for you in engaging with forgiveness. Then, commit to practice this the next time that you feel angry towards someone.

1) Physical Release

If you are a person that really enjoys physical activity and finds that it is cathartic, perhaps engage in a physical activity with more intense exertion. For example, if you like kickboxing or running practice, one of those while thinking about releasing your anger with every spurt of energy. This is not meant to ramp up your anger, but to give the energy a pathway to release from your body. Then, when you cool down, take moments of slow movement. Mindfully and intentionally begin to practice empathy toward the person you are angry with. Consider challenges that they may be facing in their life which could have caused them to treat you in a way that made you angry. If you are a spiritual person who believes in prayer or meditation, perhaps try praying for that person or doing a loving kindness meditation to send that person good energy.

2) Writing Prompt

If you are more of a writer, this activity may be for you. Take a pen and paper and let out all of your anger and resentment on the page toward this person. Let yourself be as loud and as expressive as you feel, and just let your stream of consciousness come out without trying to monitor your words. Once you have gotten all of those thoughts out, take a moment to center yourself. Perhaps that's by tuning into your breath and calming your thoughts or by attuning to the physical sensations of your body. Now shift your attention toward empathy. Think about why that person might have acted the way that they did. Think about what might be going on in their life that could be influencing their behavior toward you. Start sending them well wishes and hopes that they may find peace, solace and comfort in the challenges that they're facing through your writing . Perhaps even include some statements of gratitude for the things that you do appreciate about this person and how they benefit your workplace daily.

3) Practicing a Loving Kindness Meditation

Mentally it's often best to not even engage with any more of the negative feelings than you already have, but instead to bring awareness to yourself, your body, your breath, and as strange as it may feel, to begin to send good energy and intentions toward the person you are struggling with. There are many guided Loving Kindness meditations on free apps, YouTube and websites that you may follow and each of these can help you come to terms with your forgiveness as well as your own mental clarity and energy cleansing.

REFLECTIONS

Reflection 1

⦿ Which benefit are you most excited about?

⦿ How could these benefits result in an overall better life?

⦿ How could these changes positively impact your students?

Reflection 2

⦿ What kind of narratives about adult relationships would you like to pass on to your students?

◉ How can your modeling influence the way your students perceive the world?

◉ How could you model forgiveness for your students so that they then understand and see the benefits of releasing anger or resentment?

Reflection 3

◉ Which of the strategies resonated with you the most?

◉ Which one have you not tried that you think you could to see if it might surprise you and work well?

◉ How might you teach this strategy to a young person who is struggling with the same thing?

GENUINE

(True, unfeigned--not pretended; sincerely felt or expressed)

The Architect of the universe blessed everyone on Earth with a unique and beautiful personality. Granted, some people do act alike, but that's only in certain situations. Teachers should not contain the beauty of their particular personality but should use it to magnetize students in an effort to bring out the best in them. Teaching is extremely social. There is a constant interaction between teacher and student and vice versa. Therefore, personality plays a significant role in educating.

Before my first teaching assignment an older teacher told me to go into the classroom and not to crack a smile until the fourth nine weeks. I tried to be impersonal only opening my mouth to discipline and to teach. After the first couple of days I adopted and applied my own philosophy; which was to let my genuine personality show, I became involved in my students' lives; attending their games to support them, telling jokes to lighten the atmosphere but also remaining professional and to keep my classroom conducive to learning. Afterward, I began to love my job and the art of teaching more and more.

Teachers, allow your genuine personality to shine. Lighten the brunt of hard work through the disguise of a magnetic and unfeigned personality.

Be genuine. Be different. *Just be you*.

MENTAL HEALTH LESSON PLAN

Audience: Administrators, Educators, Central Office Personnel & Staff | **Subject:** Mental Health | **Topic:** Genuine

LESSON GOALS

Compare and contrast two case studies displaying ingenuity and genuineness in teaching.

- ◉ Explore the importance of modeling genuineness with your students.
- ◉ Consider how you can bring your most authentic self into the classroom every day.

CASEL STANDARDS

- ◉ Relationship Skills

LESSON OUTLINE

INTRODUCTION

In each workplace, a certain level of professionalism is expected. In some jobs, you are expected to wear a suit and tie to work, whereas in others you are expected to be business casual. In many workplaces, a level of professionalism with communication is expected where interactions are to be done respectfully and in a timely manner. In addition, in some professional spaces it can be considered unprofessional to share parts of your personal life with coworkers. People argue that oversharing can distract employees from the goal, which is to focus on the work in front of them.

However as an educator, perhaps some different expectations are more appropriate. Lots of cultural competency work has uncovered that the more educators can relate to their students, the more successful their students' academic outcomes. Students learn best when they feel that they can relate to their teacher, and a teacher who is only sharing the academic material with students is missing an important connection piece that brings invaluable levels of safety, joy, and relationship to the classroom.

STRATEGIES

Compare and contrast two case studies displaying ingenuity and genuineness in teaching.

Consider the most influential teachers in your life. Were these the teachers that stuck entirely to the textbook and only spoke about academics? Or were they the teachers who embedded personal stories into their teaching and shared tidbits about their hobbies and interests? Many of us would say we prefer (and actually learned from) the latter.

_____ (Now, complete Activity 1.) _____

Explore the importance of modeling genuineness with your students.

We are attracted to people who are genuine. We want to be able to see that people, even the people we admire greatly, are still flawed humans that are trying their best. When we see people in positions of power being authentic, we are reminded that even though it may seem difficult to attain their level of respect one day, that it is possible, because they're also a person just like us. Educators provide an additional sense of comfort and knowledge when they impart pieces of wisdom to their students through storytelling. That way instead of the students making certain mistakes themselves, they can learn from the mistakes of their teachers and choose more wisely.

_____ (Complete Activity 2.) _____

Consider how you can bring your most authentic self into the classroom every day.

Now, we consider how you can bring your most genuine self into the classroom. In many classrooms, students can't fathom their teachers doing anything at all outside of school. Many students joke that their teachers must sleep at the school overnight! However, we must model for students that we are also complex, dynamic people, just like they are. By incorporating what lights you up into your teaching, you are modeling for your students what joy there can be in individuality, identity, and uniqueness. This can inspire students to strive to find their true identities, hobbies, and interests.

_____ *(Now, complete Activity 3.)* _____

ACTIVITIES

1. Case Study Observation

Read the two following case studies with different ideas of how much teachers should share about their personal lives with their students.

Le'Roy is a middle school math teacher. He feels that none of his personal life should be shared with his students. He sticks to academics, and teaches every lesson exactly as his curriculum outlines for him. When he engages with his students outside of mathematics, he only asks the students questions about themselves, but never shares anything about himself with them in return. His students do not know anything about what he does outside of work or who he spends his time with, and this is what he prefers. That way, his students can focus on understanding the challenging math material and do not get distracted. Typically, Le'Roy's personality is funny, quirky, and outgoing, but he pulls all of that back in the classroom so it doesn't cause any distraction. He does not believe it is professional to show his students this side of himself.

Shania is a middle school math teacher. On the first day of the school year, Shania always tells her students the story of when she was in middle school, and how difficult she found math to be. Therefore, she explains to her students that she is on a mission to make math feel less stressful for her students, and that they should be sure to ask her questions whenever they are confused because she doesn't want anyone to feel the way she did in middle school math. She is known for being a goofy teacher who likes to sing to her students, and brings songs into memorizing math equations. She also brings her hobbies into the classroom. She is a yoga teacher, so sometimes for movement breaks, she will teach her students some yoga poses. She lets her students know that she has a partner, two older brothers, and that she loves to read when she isn't teaching. She loves to keep her students updated on her life, and made sure to tell them when her brothers got engaged to share the excitement.

2. Why does authenticity matter?

Think of the best teacher that you've ever had. Below, write their name in the middle of the space and circle it. Then, draw branches coming off of your teacher's name about things you knew about them, or learned about them as your teacher.

Now, take a moment and see if you can draw any conclusions from this activity. What did your teacher share with you that influenced your life (outside of academics)? Did you learn any life lessons? If not, did they inspire you in any way? How?

———————— (Now, complete Reflection 2.) ————————

3. Your Most Authentic Self

Describe yourself in 10 words.

Now, circle the words you think that your students already see in you.

Now, star some positive qualities you would like your students to see more of in you. How can you let this quality shine through in your teaching?

_____ (Now, complete Reflection 3.) _____

REFLECTIONS

Reflection 1

◉ Between Le'Roy and Shania, Shania's students score higher on their math exams. Why do you think that is? Why do you think Le'Roy wasn't as successful?

◉ How could you adopt a technique that Shania uses into your own teaching?

◉ How could you add your personal spin to your teaching?

Reflection 2

◉ Think about some of the key elements of your identity. How many of those do you think your students know about you?

⊙   Are there any that you could share to show them your imperfections as an adult?

⊙   What life lessons could they learn from your mistake?

Reflection 3

⊙   How can you expressing your authenticity help your students' discover theirs?

⊙   What are some things you'd be willing to share? How could these sharings benefit your students?

⊙   What are some things that would cross the line for you and feel too personal to share? Why does this piece of your identity feel this way?

HARDWORKING

(Industrious, tireless and untiring)

Educators should approach the consuming art of teaching with a passion; a zeal. They should demand and expect excellence from their students and from themselves. Hard work is completely unavoidable to a person that's trying to reach his or her maximum potential in life. Hard workers accept and understand that labor is a necessity to obtaining a successful life, so they embrace the challenge.

School districts within the Mississippi Delta serve an economically underdeveloped population. Teachers must not convince themselves to begin working hard when they have "this or that" but should optimize what they have. Napoleon Hill, American author and motivator, once instructed "Do not wait; the time will never be "just right'. Start where you stand, and work with whatever tools you may have at your command, and better tools will be found as you go along." In other words, excuses prevent hard work.

Educators should teach students about the importance and benefits of hard work. Conversely, pupils should be taught about the sacrifices they will have to make in order to fulfill the obligation to hard work. As teachers, we must tirelessly pursue excellence within our classrooms despite not having the needed tangible resources and parental support. We cannot make excuses for underperforming students and schools but must work harder in a *collective* effort. School personnel must work hard at bringing in community leaders and other stakeholders to assist with the challenges schools face. Once students observe their teachers not using excuses, they will no longer allow excuses to impede their efforts in school, and ultimately in life.

MENTAL HEALTH LESSON PLAN

Audience: Administrators, Educators, Central Office Personnel & Staff | **Subject:** Mental Health | **Topic:** Hardworking

LESSON GOALS

Reflect on your dedication to the teaching craft.

- Brainstorm how you may share the importance of hard work with your students.
- Understand the impact your modeling has on your students, and commit to transparency in your discipline.

CASEL STANDARDS

- Self-Management

LESSON OUTLINE

INTRODUCTION

If you are in the education field, you are not likely someone there for the paycheck or the public praise. You are more likely a person who pours your heart into everything you do, particularly when it pertains to the futures of young people. Regardless of how we are treated, paid, or respected, educators commit to doing extremely difficult work for the well-being of young people. We show up to work before the sun rises and leave as the sun is setting to ensure that papers are graded, seats are pushed in, and that we are prepared to teach the following day. Our job is hard work , and the truth is, we often take great pride in this hard work. It shows a passion for our craft, and a commitment to a better future. Isn't this something we want to teach to our students as well?

Of course it is. The discipline and commitment of educators is mandatory for students to receive an education that will prepare them for the ever-changing world that they are learning to enter into. We must commit to being lifelong learners, acting on well researched data, and to be attuned to the societal shifts that impact our students and how they show up in the classroom everyday . We have to be our best selves in hopes that our students leave us as their best selves.

When we share discipline and this commitment to hard work with our students, we are showing them the blueprints to a future of success regardless of the disciplines they strive to go into in order to become leaders of tomorrow. Hard work is a vital skill to attain. One of the most meaningful ways that you can teach students something is through modeling. Talking to them about hard work will often go in one ear and out the other, but if you are showing them discipline through your own actions and commitment to being successful yourself, you are giving them a clear model of a disciplined person that they may strive to be someday. As we reflect on the power of our own commitment to our work, we can see the impactful influence that discipline will then have on our students and their future paths.

Reflect on your dedication to the teaching craft.

Now, you will take the time to give yourself credit where credit is due. There are so many elements that go into a classroom running smoothly and if you are an experienced teacher, you may not even notice the intentionality, systems, and resources that you have in place in order for your students to feel successful learning in your space. Whether that is the way you set up the agenda everyday on your whiteboard, the thoughtfulness you put behind your calm corner, or the system you have for students who have missing work, you've thought carefully through each of these processes.

Then, within your own organization, you have to keep up with emails, plan lessons, and serve on committees. Often, once the school day ends, your job is not actually over. You're spending hours tutoring students or helping with after school clubs. As you begin your commute home at the end of the day, your mind and heart are not at rest as you reflect on your students, and how to better meet their needs tomorrow.

I want to remind you that you are a gift to your students and to your school community. With this activity, I hope that you can also remind yourself of how important and valued you are for the work that you put in every day.

———————— (Now, complete Activity 1.) ————————

Brainstorm how you may share the importance of hard work with your students.

As you reflect on your work ethic, you can probably think back to where that discipline originated from whether it was from the involvement in a sports team or being a lead in a theater production. Perhaps it had less to do with your involvement in certain activities and more to do with the inspirational people that you had to look up to. Maybe this was a parent who worked several jobs to make sure that your family was provided for, or a celebrity you idolized who inspired you to do the work that you are now pursuing. To help students understand the importance of hard work, you have to relate to them directly. Their inspiration around work ethic will be unique for each student. Therefore, in this activity, we will think about ways we can connect each student to their own personal reason why discipline is so important to them.

Understand the impact your modeling has on your students, and commit to transparency with them in some form.

If you ask many students what they think teachers do outside of work, they can go blank with a confused expression. They may only see you in your work environment, and therefore, find it difficult to imagine you out in the real world. As educators, one of the most impactful ways that we can teach students is through modeling. Therefore, the intentionality you have in how your students see you is really impactful. They see you when you look tired, but drink your coffee and teach all your lessons anyway. They see you after school, still grading those papers. They see your car still in the parking lot well after the school day.

This isn't a call to put on a show for your students or be anything you aren't in front of them, but to perhaps be more transparent in the commitment you have to their success. When you grade for several hours on the weekend, perhaps mention that to them. If you have to stay at school in professional development while they go home for a half day, let them know what you're working on that afternoon and what you're excited to learn. Again, this isn't to make them feel bad, but to show them the thoughtfulness and the commitment that you have to their success in school.

(Now, complete Activity 3.)

ACTIVITIES

1. Your Dedication to The Craft

This next activity may feel a little tedious , but as an educator, we know that you will not shy away from the little bit of extra work. Thinking about your average school day, write bullet points of every task you do from the beginning to the end of the day from when you enter the school building to when you exit it. This includes making copies, meeting with your coach, and feel free to include some of the tasks that we don't plan for throughout the school day. These include teaching coping skills to the student who is extremely anxious for their test, to finding missing work for a student on the spot, to a surprise observation from admin. As you develop this bulleted list, notice the impact that each of these actions have on your students.

_____ (Now, complete Reflection 1.) _____

Importance of Hard Work Exploration

Now it's time for you to put on your teacher hat. For many people we are driven by a role model we look up to and want to become like. Others feel inspired by a certain career goal or achievement that we are determined to reach in the future. If you were teaching your class about how they might connect to their "why" around hard work , you would likely model by doing this activity yourself. So that is what we are going to do together now.

Answer the following questions.

Determine which of these things motivate you the most . Is it looking up to a role model? The desire to achieve a certain goal? The hope to influence everlasting change?

Now, describe this motivator and how it's inspired you and how you show up each day.

Think about the best version of yourself that has reached your fullest potential. What should you continue to do or stop doing in order to become this most fulfilled version of yourself?

When you work with your students to do this activity, you can ask them these same questions and share your reflections with them.

————————— (Now, complete Reflection 2.) —————————

2. Modeling Discipline Transparently

A lot of young people are out of touch with how much work it takes to be successful in the workplace, especially one that requires constant flexibility, focus, and an intricate balance of several elements in order to run smoothly. We all know those students who sigh when it took a little too long to get their graded quiz returned back to them or the students who come to you at the very last minute asking for a recommendation. In some cases, you may seem superhuman to your students. However in many cases, they don't have a full grasp of the level of commitment that teachers have in order to have a successful classroom environment each day. Therefore, modeling the level of intentionality and work that goes into their learning environment can be necessary in order to show them discipline and intentionality in an environment they exist in every day.

Think of some ways you can be transparent around the level of thought and work that you put into your teaching. We want to be mindful of this so that it doesn't sound like you are complaining or that you are irritated by this level of work, but instead are sharing the truth that goes into the day-to-day role of teaching. You can mention how you are in a graduate program to help you become a better teacher at night. Perhaps mention how you are working on making the student council election process and how excited you are to share information with students. Let them see your humanness through your hard work . Below, brainstorm four ways you can share your intentionality with your students.

————————— (Now, complete Reflection 3.) —————————

REFLECTIONS

Reflection 1

- ⊙ What is your first thought after writing down each task you do throughout the school day?

_____

_____

_____

◉ How many of these tasks had you planned ahead of time? How many were thrown on your plate in the middle of the day?

◉ Take a moment to really look at this list and take a deep breath. What feelings come up when you review these tasks ? Does this stir up any feelings toward other people?

◉ **Reflection 2**

◉ Why do you feel that it is important to model this thought process in front of your students?

◉ What thoughts and feelings come up when you explore the steps you should be taking to reach this goal?

◉ Do you feel like you're on track or do you feel like there is a lot of progress to be made?

◉ **Reflection 3**

- How does sharing your good work ethic with your students feel to you? Is it you already do, or is it completely foreign to you?

- Why do you think students seeing your intentionality could positively impact them?

- What do you think they will learn from your clear modeling of hard work?

I

IDEALISTIC

(High-minded; of high moral or intellectual value)

Teachers should impress students with their intellectual value, thus making students actively desire to learn more. Being equipped with the intellectual ability to synthesize course content and to solve complex problems is a prerequisite for teachers. A classroom is a plethora of differing views, attitudes and more importantly learning styles. As most of you have learned in your teaching career, every student is different and thus learns differently. Here are a few suggestions for becoming an idealistic teacher:

1. Submerge yourself in your field by becoming a member of a professional organization.
2. Attend workshops and conferences networking and exchange ideas with other educators.
3. Read the latest research pertaining to child development and student learning.
4. Daily, designate time to yourself to think and reflect on what you have done and how you can do it better.
5. Think outside the box.

Being idealistic and teaching differently will be very challenging when low scores on high-stakes testing are forcing the state of Mississippi to take over school districts; however, you must explore your creative side to reach every learning style within a classroom. The task is difficult, but you just read about HARD WORK on the previous page.

MENTAL HEALTH LESSON PLAN

Audience: Administrators, Educators, Central Office Personnel & Staff

Subject: Mental Health

Topic: Idealistic

LESSON GOALS

Determine how you can become the most idealistic version of yourself as an educator.

- ◉ Be honest with yourself about what you can commit to, and make a plan to do just that.
- ◉ Practice tapping into your creativity in order to best serve the range of students in your classroom.

CASEL STANDARDS

- ◉ Relationship Skills

LESSON OUTLINE

INTRODUCTION

Realistically in teaching, you are never going to reach a level of experience or expertise that indicates crossing a finish line. An excellent educator constantly learns, innovates, and adjusts based on the needs of their classroom. The more a teacher is able to do this, the more receptive your students will be to the concepts you are trying to teach them. To be an educator that is truly dedicated to your craft, you must think of teaching outside of the realm of your job description in order to adapt to the way that the world is changing and education is evolving. You must be tuned into the latest research, the newest teaching skills, and the methods that your students will respond most enthusiastically to. Just as you are teaching your students to be, you need to commit to also being a lifelong learner. As much as your students are constantly learning in your space , you should be learning how to better your craft.

In reality, there is a limit to what we as educators have the energy and capacity to do. But do not ignore those sparks of inspiration that come up whether you are reading an interesting article on Facebook, or hearing about the work an innovative educator is doing in your professional development. Follow that curiosity to see how these pieces of knowledge can improve your teaching.

It is also no mystery that every student in your classroom requires something different in order to access content. Therefore, it is extremely beneficial for you to really know the young people in front of you and to be creative in your approaches so that every child can be successful in your room.

Determine how you can become the most idealistic version of yourself as an educator.

First, we are going to brainstorm how you can become your most successful self as an educator. Don't feel intimidated by this list that you create, because as I will remind you no teacher will ever be perfect and there is no finish line to cross. You can, however, always take small steps toward becoming a better educator for your students. Whether this is truly reading educator emails that are in your junk inbox , committing to a live Zoom with some leaders in the education field, or finding and advocating to go to a professional development conference , these steps toward your own development will spark and inspire your continued love and commitment to your craft. In the first activity, you will think of some of the ways to tune into opportunities that are already available to you that you just need to start saying yes to.

_____   (Now, complete Activity 1.)   _____

Be honest with yourself about what you can commit to, and make a plan to do just that.

We would like to say we will do all of these things in an idealistic world, but you don't actually live in an idealistic world. Therefore, you need to decide which you can actually commit to based on your current workload, the commitments in your personal life, and your personal career goals. In the next activity, you will pick one of these professional development investments and make a plan so that you can commit to this work moving forward.

_____   (Complete Activity 2.)   _____

Practice tapping into your creativity in order to best serve the range of students in your classroom.

Now, we will shift our focus to the students in your classroom. Another key component to being the best teacher that you can be is understanding the diversity of needs that live in your classroom everyday. Every student learns in a different way and is responsive to different methods of teaching. Therefore, doing the same lecture-style everyday or working in groups four out of five days of the week will probably not work for every learner in your space. Therefore, you will think about the different types of learners in your classroom and how you might teach them a concept from the subject you already teach.

(Now, complete Activity 3.)

ACTIVITIES

1. Saying Yes to Your Development

Take a moment to consider some of the professional opportunities that have been presented to you that you have not yet taken advantage of. If you don't feel you have access to these opportunities already, brainstorm some ways to find how you can connect to communities that spark your interest in your own continued development.

_____ (Now, complete Reflection 1.) _____

2. Realistic Commitment

Now it's time for us to be honest with ourselves. Write down the opportunity that excites you, inspires you, and could actually fit into your already very busy life.

Think about how much time you can honestly invest into this commitment: is it taking an hour-and-a-half once a month to read research articles? Is it going to one professional development a year? Is it committing to listening to one education-based podcast? Make sure that it feels manageable and exciting to add into your already packed schedule.

Lastly, pencil it in. Whether it needs to be in your agenda, a reminder in your outlook , or typed into your phone calendar, make it a tangible task to check off like your other commitments.

_____ (Now, complete Reflection 2.) _____

3. Serving Every Student

Make a list of each student in your class. Then, label each student with one of four choices based on what you know about them.

1. Write a 'V' next to their name if you believe that the student is a visual learner.

2. Write a 'D' next to your student's name if you believe that they learn best by doing, for example by using manipulatives or getting active with their learning.

3. Write an 'A' next to the student's name if you believe that they are an auditory learner and learn best through storytelling or through hearing you explain the content out loud.

4. Write a 'C' next to your students you believe learn best by collaborating with their peers and engaging with questions and answers with you as their teacher.

Now, write down a specific skill in your subject area you need to teach or have already taught your students.

In the space below, brainstorm how you could present this skill to your students differently, keeping in mind the needs of all the different learners in your space. Is there some way that you could tie in all four learning styles to reach every student within that lesson?

———————————— *(Now, complete Reflection 3.)* ————————————

REFLECTIONS

Reflection 1

◉ Do any of these opportunities excite you?

◉ Do you have any ideas to develop your craft outside of what has already been offered to you?

◉ How could investing in one of these opportunities better your practice in the classroom, and for yourself professionally?

Reflection 2

◉ How did it feel going from the idealistic list to the realistic one?

◉ How do you feel toward your new commitment?

◉ Are you looking forward to adding it to your life? If not, perhaps take another look at your commitment and edit it to your liking.

Reflection 3

How can you take this process, and make it more manageable for lesson planning each day?

⦿ How can you ensure your teaching is accessible to each student every day?

⦿ Reflect on which students you tend to accommodate the most in your teaching style. How can you include your students who aren't as aligned with your teaching style more intentionally?

JOYFUL

(Elated; full of high-spirited delight)

Find delight in educating. Enjoy going to work. Wake up every morning giving thanks to the Most High and accept today's failures and successes even before stepping out the bed. Problems are a reality in life, and to think otherwise is setting yourself up for an abundant supply of disappointments. You may be asking, "Why should I be joyful about going to work? I have bad students?" That may be your situation, but you shouldn't let any person steal your joy. Indeed, poorly managed children can take a toll on an optimistic attitude, but schools have mechanisms in place for misbehaving children, so continually referring them to the principal, counselor or any other agency your school has in place. Below are two reasons why you should be joyous when teaching:

1. You have invested thousands of dollars in yourself by obtaining a license to teach.
2. You have invested countless hours studying and preparing yourself to teach.

The significance is you have invested too much money and too much time preparing yourself for the position you currently occupy. Essentially, you are living your dreams because you are doing what you set out to do.

A STORY

One teacher was so angry and frustrated with the problems of ABC High School that she decided to transfer to XYZ High School. However, after a few weeks at her new high school she began to notice problems.

Be joyous! Embrace your present school and its problems because the school you may transfer to will have its own problems as well.

MENTAL HEALTH LESSON PLAN

Audience: Administrators, Educators, Central Office Personnel & Staff   **Subject:** Mental Health   **Topic:** Joyful

LESSON GOALS

Reflect on teachers' "why" for choosing teaching.

- Learn to notice the joyful moments in the workplace.
- Develop strategies to remind teachers of joyful moments.

CASEL STANDARDS

- Self-Awareness

LESSON OUTLINE

INTRODUCTION

Teachers are tasked with many responsibilities that people in other workplaces do not have. A particularly unique one is to lead environments that young people grow up in. A wonderful part of childhood is the special sense of joy that many children feel as they discover new things in a nurturing environment. As teachers, we hope to make spaces that are joyful in order to cultivate a love of learning. This becomes a particularly challenging task as you recognize all of the many other responsibilities that teachers juggle. However, when teachers are deeply rooted in their "why", they will be reminded of the value of finding joy in learning spaces.

It is natural for us to latch on to negative encounters instead of positive ones. However, we can adapt our way of thinking so that we notice more positivity. The more conscientious we are about noticing the positive, the more likely we will feel positively as well. If we are noticing and actively looking for joy we are more likely to feel it ourselves. In this lesson we will look at how to make the classroom feel truly joyful by reflecting on why we returned to it as teachers, how to notice the sparks of joy, and how to remember them during more difficult moments.

Reflect on the "why" behind choosing the teaching career path..

First, we are going to think about why we became educators in the first place. Many of us went into teaching because a great teacher taught us and inspired us. Some others, like myself, went into teaching because their experiences in school were not positive. Therefore, they are trying to allow other children to feel safe and nurtured in their education space. It's likely that when you decided to be a teacher you had lofty goals. Whether that was how beautifully designed your classroom would be, or how much work you would actually get done during your prep, you likely saw teaching through rose colored glasses. You believed that stepping into a role as an educator would be a positive change in your life. In the following activity you are going to describe how your role as an educator could bring positive change to yourself, your students, and the world.

(Now, complete Activity 1.)

1. **Notice the joyful moments in the workplace.**

Next we're going to train ourselves to notice the joy in our everyday work. Even on a day where you are exhausted, struggling, and just ready for that end of school bell to ring, there are countless pockets of magic happening throughout your school building. In a place meant for learning and nurturing students, there are sure to be many moments of that happening. We just have to notice. In the following activity, you will think about places of joy that you might be missing or not paying attention to during your work day.

2. Develop strategies to remind teachers of joyful moments.

Now, let's get really specific about how we can notice more joy during our work day. Two of my favorite ways to do this are really simple and really effective. The first is increasing your positive feelings by keeping track of moments where people say something nice to you in particular via email. Any time you are having a hard moment at work, you can open this folder and remind yourself of some moments that made you smile. Once you read a few of these emails, you will feel some more gratitude and positivity toward teaching.

(Now, complete Activity 3.)

ACTIVITIES

3. "Why" Reflection

In the space below, you will jot down some words of the good things you hoped teaching would bring to yourself, your students, and to the world.

Yourself

Your Students

_____

_____

_____

The World

_____

_____

_____

_____

————————— (Now, complete Reflection 1.) —————————

1.   Notice the Joy

In the space below, think of one to three joyful moments that are most prominent in your memory from your teaching career. If you can't think of any, move on to the next prompt.

_____

_____

In the space below, bullet three to five times during the school day when joyful moments could happen either between students, between teachers, or in student and teacher interactions.

_____

_____

Now take a moment to sit back in your chair, ground your feet into the floor, and perhaps close your eyes. Visualize the beginning of your work day. You hear footsteps rushing up the stairs and your first few students walk in the room greeting you with a big smile and wave. They excitedly chat with one another as you get ready for your first class. One of them compliments you on your outfit and another one asks how you are doing. As you visualize this scene, look around and think of some moments that perhaps you are missing in your classroom. Are there some students working on a card for someone out sick? Did someone draw a very cute picture on your whiteboard? Consider the in-betweens. At your own pace, take yourself through your school day and really notice those moments of joy that you might have missed before. Once your visualized day has ended you may open your eyes and work on reflection questions for Activity 2.

_____ (Now, complete Reflection 2.) _____

2. Joyful Strategies

In your email, make a folder where you just click and drag any email that makes you smile throughout your day. Maybe this is a teacher that was complimenting you for your strong work, maybe this is a student emailing you a movie recommendation, or maybe this is your boss giving you a shout out. Whatever it is, anything that makes you smile can be clicked and dragged into this folder.

Now, any time you are having a hard moment at work, feel free to open up this folder and remind yourself of some moments that made you smile. Look through a few of these emails and likely in a few minutes, you will feel some more gratitude and positivity toward teaching.

The second strategy is really similar to the first, but instead you find a place to keep track of things your students have said that make you smile. Maybe it's a silly story they told that made you laugh, or maybe it's a moment that helped you feel like you were making a difference. Whatever it is, find a way to keep track of it. I have a note on my phone where I keep track of all of these comments. I love to look through these when I'm feeling drained or exhausted by teaching.

REFLECTIONS

Reflection 1

- Where have your hopes come true in yourself, your students, and the world?

- Is there more here than you notice or remember on a day to day basis? Why do you think that is?

- How could you be thoughtful about places to bring more joy into teaching?

Reflection 2

- What came up for you in this visualization practice?

- What did you learn from it?

- How can you take this learning with you into your next work day?

Reflection 3

- How does it feel to receive simple strategies to find joy in hard moments?

- Do these strategies feel practical? If not, how can you remind yourself of the joyful moments instead?

- How do you think reminding yourself of these moments could impact your day?

KIND-HEARTED

(Having or proceeding from an innately kind disposition)

Plato, a Greek author and philosopher, once stated, "Be kind, for everyone you meet is fighting a hard battle." Even though Plato lived over fifteen hundred years ago his words are still true. Successful people, including educators know this fact. Therefore they try to treat everyone how they would want to be treated;—respectfully. Teachers should be kind to their pupils, because many of them are trapped in unstable home environments beyond their control. As thinkers we must understand that within our classrooms there are frightened children afraid of going back home to an abusive alcoholic parent. We must accept the possibility that some of our students are infected or have a loved one with HIV/AIDS; the Mississippi Delta has a high average of HIV/AIDS cases. Should we pamper them and let them take advantage of our kindness? No! But amongst all the darkness they deal with on a daily basis we must be light. We owe it to ourselves as much as we owe it to them.

ASSIGNMENT

1. Say "yes" when you want to say "no."

2. Say something kind to a person that looks like he/she needs encouraging words.

3. Perform three acts of kindness tomorrow at work. (Make sure it's something outside your job description.)

Be kind for kindness sake.

MENTAL HEALTH LESSON PLAN

Audience: Administrators, Educators, Central Office Personnel & Staff

Subject: Mental Health

Topic: Kindhearted

LESSON GOALS

Practice leaning in when people at work push your limits.

- Brainstorm kind words you can share with someone at work.
- Decide three kind acts you will perform the following work day.

CASEL STANDARDS

- Self-Awareness

LESSON OUTLINE

INTRODUCTION

It's very unlikely that you have become a teacher without also being kind-hearted. So this lesson is not assuming anything other than that. However, it is reminding you to make choices that are kind-hearted even in moments when you may feel ready to snap. This could be with your students, your coworkers, or your coach. In addition, the more that you spread positivity the more positivity will return to you. Therefore, we will also practice intentional moments of kindness that will not only make another person feel good, but will also help you feel good in return.

STRATEGIES

Practice leaning in when people at work push your limits.

One way that we can practice being more kind-hearted at work is by leaning into saying yes when we want to say no. In moments where you could have a short fuse, we encourage you to practice grace. Frustrations can come from many different people as a teacher. They could come from parents, students or coworkers. In this activity we will practice looking at our gut reaction vs. considering a more kind response.

_____ (Now, complete Activity 1.) _____

Brainstorm kind words you can share with someone at work.

Now we are going to consider how we can bring more kindness into the workplace. Typically when you receive encouragement or a kind word, you are more likely to feel better. When you share those kind words with others, you can change someone else's day for the better. In the next activity, will think about how you can do so.

_____ (Complete Activity 2.) _____

Decide three kind acts you will perform the following work day.

Similar to our last strategy, now we are going to consider three things that we can do that bring more kindness to our work community. Maybe you can go out of your way to do a favor for someone or do something that makes your students feel especially loved. Consider this in the next activity.

ACTIVITIES

1. **Say "yes" when you want to say "no."**

    In the space below, you will read two different scenarios. First, write down your gut reaction and the response that your instinct wants to give. Then, write a more kind-hearted and wise response to the situation.

    Your student asks to go to the bathroom and is gone for 10 minutes. You look out in the hallway and they are nowhere to be found. You call them over the loudspeaker, and finally your student returns to your classroom. Now you're going to speak to your student.

    What's your gut reaction?

    ⊙ What's a kinder way to respond to the situation?

Your coworker asked you to email her about an important situation that you need her help with. You sent a detailed email in a timely manner and are hoping for a prompt response. Three days go by, and you still have not received a response. Now you need to contact her to follow up about this email.

⊙ What is your unfiltered gut reaction?

⊙ What's a more kind way to go about this?

_____

_____

_____ *(Now, complete Reflection 1.)* _____

2. Saying Kind Words

Think of three people you appreciate at work. List them below.

_____

_____

_____

Now, think of a compliment you can share with that person or a way of expressing gratitude for how they show up every day. List them next to their names, and make sure you share these kind words with the people you chose this week at work.

_____ *(Now, complete Reflection 2.)* _____

Acts of Kindness

Below, list three ways that you can bring more kindness to school tomorrow. This could be a favor or just a way of making someone else feel special.

_____

_____

_____

REFLECTIONS

Reflection 1

◉ What did you learn from this exercise?

◉ What are some ways you can stop yourself in a moment of irritability, so you can think of a kinder response?

◉ How could your reaction influence a situation when it's negative? When it's positive?

Reflection 2

◉ Why did you choose these people?

◉ Why do you appreciate them?

◉ How could your kind words affect how they feel for the rest of the day?

KIND-HEARTED

Reflection 3

- Looking at the acts of kindness that you brainstormed, are these things that you do normally? If not, why not?

_____

_____

- How can these kind acts fit into your already very busy day?

_____

_____

- How can you show the people around you that you care about them while also nurturing yourself?

_____

_____

LOVING

(Enjoy; getting pleasure from)

Love is an extremely deep emotion that embodies your affection for a particular object. Usually when a person loves something he/she puts their all into it and they enjoy doing it. Teachers that love the act of teaching let it consume them. They offer after-school tutoring classes, they grade papers within a decent timeframe and they show up to work early and daily with a positive attitude because they feel as though they are serving a purpose.

In a 2007 Conference Board report obtained by MSNBC it cited that less than 39 percent of young workers (25 and under) was satisfied with their jobs. It elaborated "Workers age 45 to 54 have the second lowest level of satisfaction (less than 45 percent)." Fortunately, the feeling of loving your job can be acquired, but first you have to examine your thoughts to find out why you dislike it. Once you have identified the reasons you dislike your job begin to resolve those issues internally. However, if the reasons are not intrapersonal then you may need to address or accept the negative influences; but in the end *you must not give power to them.*

Simple suggestions on growing to love your job:

1. Find purpose in the challenge of work.
2. Become comfortable in the area you teach.
3. Create friendships with staff and faculty.
4. Have fun at work.

MENTAL HEALTH LESSON PLAN

Audience: Administrators, Educators, Central Office Personnel & Staff   **Subject:** Mental Health   **Topic:** Loving

LESSON GOALS

Consider your students' needs and how you can approach them more lovingly in challenging moments.

- ○ Plan intentional moments for connection.
- ○ Brainstorm how to make your workplace more joyful.

CASEL STANDARDS

- ○ Self-Management

LESSON OUTLINE

INTRODUCTION

Aside from parents and caregivers, teachers are the adults that spend the most time with students. We have a tremendous impact on their moods, their perspectives, and their days. When we approach students with love, grace, and positivity, they are more likely to have a great day. In some situations, a teacher may be the only loving adult in a student's life. Sometimes it can feel difficult to move with love, especially when our job feels really difficult. However, by responding to students lovingly, planning intentional moments of connection, and making our workplace more joyful, it will feel easier to move with love.

STRATEGIES

Consider your students' needs and how you can approach them more lovingly in challenging moments.

It is no surprise that students can be really challenging sometimes. Whether you are dealing with tantrums, attitudes, or lack of motivation, this can feel frustrating for the teacher to deal with every day. However, just like these behaviors may be impacting you, something is bothering your students, which is causing them to behave this way. They might have a challenging situation happening at home, some trouble with anxiety, or be dealing with friendship drama. Try to remember in these moments how you might've reacted when you were their age. Although you may have a better perspective as an adult, make sure that you approach students with empathy and love when they are facing something difficult.

(Now, complete Activity 1.)

Plan intentional moments for connection.

People often underestimate the power of connection. Having positive relationships with other people supports good mental health. Not to mention, it makes daily work feel so much better! When you form positive connections with the people around you, work feels a lot less burdensome. These connections can be with your coworkers, administration, and your students. Being intentional about these connections can help you approach each day more lovingly.

(Complete Activity 2.)

Brainstorm how to make your workplace more joyful.

Now is where we sprinkle in the joy. Consider where you work and where you spend most of your time throughout the day. For many of us, that is likely in our classroom and at our desk. Are there intentional items in these spaces that bring you joy? Do you enjoy being in that space? If not, it's time to reassess.

ACTIVITIES

1. **Practice empathy.**

   In the space below, you will read a few different scenarios. From a centered place, think of a loving response to each situation. Think of how you would want to be talked to when you were a child in this situation.

   ⦿ You are working at your desk, and look up to see a student standing on a chair. She becomes unsteady on her feet and falls down. Now, your student is crying and has hurt herself.

   ⦿ A student skipped your tutoring session. Now, he is taking your test, and has a lot of questions about the material.

   ⦿ Two students are pushing each other at recess.

   ⦿ You find out that several students have been taking other students' milk every day at lunch.

(Now, complete Reflection 1.)

2. Caring for Connection

It can be easy to want to keep your head down at work, get your job done, and rush home. In order to ensure that you are teaching from a loving place, prioritize positive interactions with the people around you.

Think of 3 people you will go out of your way to connect with positively the next school day. List them below and an idea of what you can talk about next to their names.

(Now, complete Reflection 2.)

3. Joyful Workplace

Below, you are going to think of 5 ways you can bring more joy into your space. This could include taking care of the clutter that's been piling up for months, adding a fun new keyboard, or bringing in your favorite plant from home. Think of what would make you enjoy the space more, and commit to making these small changes! With the amount of time you spend at work, these tweaks will make a huge difference.

REFLECTIONS

Reflection 1

⊙   Why is it difficult to respond lovingly to some of these situations?

⊙   How can you care for yourself so you are able to respond from a loving place each time?

⊙   How might your students benefit from your loving response?

Reflection 2

⊙   What feelings came up for you when you thought about these moments of connection?

⊙   How might these impact your day?

⊙   Why is prioritizing connection helpful to move from a place of love?

Reflection 3

◉   Notice how your feelings shifted after that brainstorm. Why do you think that is?

◉   Think of how you can design your workplace with a similar intentionality to your home.

◉   How might this shift your feelings toward work?

MOTIVATOR

(A positive motivational influence)

Effective teachers know the power of persuasion or the ability to motivate themselves and students into performing tiring acts. Mastering the skill of motivation is a unique tool that can be utilized to bring out the best in yourself and your students. Motivating is voicing positive words and performing deeds of service. Anyone can exploit a person's weaknesses but few can enhance a person's strength. Influential educators choose to build instead of breaking, and to assist instead of neglecting. Motivational teachers are the people that encourage students to push themselves, so that they can exceed the greatest obstacles.

Every teacher will not be able to give a momentous speech roaring students to success; however, teachers can motivate students by opening their imagination; teachers can arouse the desire to learn by designing challenging lessons. When I asked a college class to identify one problem that hinders success in the Mississippi Delta the majority stated "the lack of motivation in classrooms." So as educators, what type of "carrot" must we place in students' line of vision? When we teach our children are we challenging them to explore the depths of their thought? Do we become satisfied because they were able to recall facts, or as Bloom asks "are we willing to push them to apply, analyze, synthesize, evaluate, and create?"

Motivating students to learn more should be the goal of every teacher, principal and parent. Professional development funds must be used to explore new and exciting methods of pushing students to success.

MENTAL HEALTH LESSON PLAN

Audience: Administrators, Educators, Central Office Personnel & Staff

Subject: Mental Health

Topic: Motivator

LESSON GOALS

Determine how to find your students' spark.

- ○ Practice communicating high expectations from a place of love.
- ○ Brainstorm your motivation tactics and incorporate in the FUN!

CASEL STANDARDS

- ○ Relationship Skills

LESSON OUTLINE

INTRODUCTION

I don't know about you, but when I remember my experiences in school,, especially in the older grades, I remember feeling bored, tired, and spaced out. There were so many other things on my mind besides the academic material, that it often felt really difficult to focus on what was in front of me. Whether you are the best teacher in the world or not, there are days where your students will feel unmotivated. As their teacher, one of the many parts of the job is getting your students excited about the learning you do together. Whether this is through personal connection, high expectations, or being their biggest cheerleader, your students need your high spirit to reach their fullest potential in the classroom.

STRATEGIES

Determine how to find your students' spark.

Great teachers really take the time and energy to know and love their students. The more you learn about them, the better you will understand their goals, their dreams, and what makes them feel most empowered. Therefore, it is up to you to take what you know about your students and use that to their advantage as a way to motivate them when they're feeling discouraged.

(Now, complete Activity 1.)

Practice communicating high expectations from a place of love.

Some teachers are strict with their students to show power, or simply because they expect them to behave a certain way. We've all had that scary teacher who made us anxious in class, which never felt truly helpful. There's a way that you can communicate high expectations with your students while also always coming from a place of love.

(Complete Activity 2.)

Brainstorm your motivation tactics and incorporate the FUN!

Students learn the most when they are engaged. Students are the most engaged when lessons are FUN! By bringing in positive reinforcement, friendly competition, and hands-on activities, you can help the learning environment feel more alive and motivating for your students.

(Now, complete Activity 3.)

ACTIVITIES

1. **Determine how to find your students' spark.**

Consider a student that you don't know as well as your other students. Then, list the things that you do know about that student.

Next, think of a way that you can get to know your student's 'spark' or what motivates them most. Commit to it the following week, getting a better idea of what that spark is, and connecting with your student around that topic.

(Now, complete Reflection 1.)

1. **Practice communicating high expectations from a place of love.**

Next, we will practice writing statements that communicate high expectations and care for our students. Write at least three below!

Example: Yes we have homework, because you are brilliant and need to build those brain muscles!

(Now, complete Reflection 2.)

1. **Brainstorm your motivation tactics and incorporate the FUN!**

How do you want to bring your lessons to life? Through games, competition, and hands -on activities? Brainstorm below.

Now, plan out the details. Think of a specific lesson, and exactly how you plan to make this a motivating and positive experience for your students. Get creative and have fun!

(Now, complete Reflection 3.)

REFLECTIONS

Reflection 1

- What was your spark in school? What motivated you?

- Did any teachers ever use your spark to motivate you?

- If not, how would that have made you feel?

Reflection 2

- Did you have any teachers who showed both care and a commitment to high expectations?

◉ How did you know?

◉ If not, how do you think that would have helped your perspectives about learning?

Reflection 3

◉ Was joy intentionally brought into your learning space?

◉ What might motivation and fun do to your students' experience?

◉ What are you excited about?

NURTURING

(Rear, raise; help develop, help grow)

A student's twenty-four hour day can be divided into 3 equal sums:

1. Eight hours of sleep
2. Eight hours attending school and
3. Eight hours at home.

Students spend the exact amount of time at school and at home. Effective teachers understand that they are more than educators; they are doctors when students need medical attention; they are motivators when students are depressed or when they're unable to grasp concepts; they are counselors when students are going through problems; teachers are the parents of students one-third of the day; teachers are nurtures willing to assist in the developmental process of the youth. Developing children into productive citizens the world's workforce can use to fill the void that Nature will make. To effectively nurture, teachers must offer optimal feedback on student's work otherwise there is no growth.

Below are three nurturing tips that will be useful in developmental process:

1. Supply a rubric. How the teacher will grade should not be a secret. Teachers should supply ample directions along with a detailed rubric of what they wish to see.
2. Understanding of assignment. Students should know the purpose of the assignment other than to receive a grade. They should be told how the assignment benefits them and how it can be applied practically.
3. Effective feedback is crucial. Teachers must supply timely feedback on submitted assignments. When returning assignments teachers must highlight the students' perfections and flaws.

MENTAL HEALTH LESSON PLAN

Audience: Administrators, Educators, Central Office Personnel & Staff

Subject: Mental Health   Topic: Nurturing

LESSON GOALS

Determine the ways teachers can nurture their students.

- ○ Practice providing rationale for the "why" behind learning.
- ○ Provide supportive feedback.

CASEL STANDARDS

- ○ Relationship Skills

LESSON OUTLINE

INTRODUCTION

Among the many important roles that educators have is the responsibility to care for our students every day. In the classroom, intentional care can look really different depending on the personal needs of a student, the objectives for the day, and the necessity to help students achieve academic goals. There are many ways that we as educators can nurture our students. Sometimes this is by checking in with a student who seems unusually down. Other times, this is providing very clear directions for the important term paper. Often, this is holding students to high expectations while also supporting them in developing the confidence to reach those expectations. In this lesson, we are going to look at the many ways we can nurture our students, think about the importance of providing strong rationale to our students, and practice providing feedback that communicates high expectations as well as care and support.

STRATEGIES

Determine the ways teachers can nurture their students.

A beautiful thing about getting to know your students is learning how each individual needs to be supported in the classroom. Some students want to feel challenged and motivated. Others can't begin to learn from you until they first trust you. It's a really wonderful and challenging part of the job. By carefully considering the uniqueness of every student that you come across, you can get a sense of how differently you should nurture each one of them.

(Now, complete Activity 1.)

Practice providing rationale for the "why" behind learning.

Something that teachers can often forget is to provide a rationale for why you ask students to do certain things. If you are a teacher, you are very familiar with the question, "but why?" and we want to be really careful about truly responding to this question. If we do not provide an intentional response, we risk the teacher-student dynamic becoming a bit of a power struggle. We never want to fall into the trap of saying, "because I said so." Our students' futures and the opportunities that education can provide for them need to be central to our rationale every day for students to see the meaning behind their work in the classroom.

(Complete Activity 2.)

Provide supportive feedback.

A central aspect of nurturing student growth is providing meaningful feedback. Something that students will inevitably experience for the rest of their lives is receiving feedback and learning how to use it to help them grow. Teachers can often become so used to providing feedback that it can become direct and concise without actually feeling supportive. We have to keep in mind that students can be really sensitive to the tone in which we give that feedback. Therefore, we want to be clear, constructive, and encouraging.

ACTIVITIES

Determine the ways teachers can nurture their students.

Make a list of 5 – 8 of your students.

Now next to each of their names, write a way that you can nurture that individual student based on what you know about their personality, needs, and motivations.

(Now, complete Reflection 1.)

Practice providing rationale for the "why" behind learning.

There are certain things that students ask us, "but why," about that are particularly challenging to respond to with clear reasoning. Practice responding with clear rationale to some of the questions below.

"But why...

Do we have to do homework?

Do we need to ask to go to the bathroom?

Do I need to write my homework in my agenda?

_____

_____

Do I need to write this paper?

_____

_____

_____

——————————— *(Now, complete Reflection 2.)* ———————————

Provide supportive feedback.

In the following scenarios, respond with feedback that is both constructive AND supportive. On the first blank respond with something constructive, and on the second blank add in your support.

_____

_____

Your student bombed their math text, clearly not understanding how to find the slope of a line.

_____ & _____

Your student missed three days of school and is asking for the work that they missed.

_____ & _____

Your student is having a hard time determining how to use appropriate punctuation in their essays.

_____ & _____

REFLECTIONS

Reflection 1

◉   What stood out to you about this activity?

◉   How does this shift your thinking about nurturing your students?

◉   How can you ensure that you are also nurturing yourself with all of these needs in your classroom?

Reflection 2

◉   How can clear rationale impact your students?

- ◉ What do you have to answer "but why" to the most in your classroom?

- ◉ How can you respond with thoughtful rationale?

Reflection 3

- ◉ Which piece of feedback came more naturally to you?

- ◉ What can be a better time to give feedback verbally instead of written?

- ◉ Does your feedback provide a clear next step on how to move forward?

ORGANIZED

(Prepare, devise; systematic planning)

Nothing great has ever been maintained without organization. Being organized can surely move a school in a positive direction. Principals and teachers must work together for the improvement of their students. Extreme organization on all levels is the key. Record books must be kept current, reflecting daily assignments. A system of rewarding students must be established and adhered to by students and administration. A uniform code of rules and consequences has to be posted on every classroom wall, and must be followed through with when broken. Classrooms must be organized and orderly and lesson must be thoroughly planned.

When parents request a child's assignments teachers shouldn't be scrounging through tons of unorganized papers. That is surely one sign that you're unorganized and unprepared. Instead, when parents request assignments teachers should pull out the student's file and present it to the parent. Utilizing a file cabinet in a classroom is a great asset and will prevent many headaches. During my first years of teaching I taught six different classes and kept all the papers together at the bottom of my desk in a towering stack. I had the hardest time searching through the mountain of paper trying to locate a particular assignment. I quickly learned from that mistake and begin to color code the classes and begin logging them in a file cabinet.

Organization is a must in any organization.

MENTAL HEALTH LESSON PLAN

Audience: Administrators, Educators, Central Office Personnel & Staff   **Subject:** Mental Health   **Topic:** Organized

LESSON GOALS

Analyze current systems in your classroom to either keep or change.

- Determine a positive reinforcement system for your students.
- Assess personal organization system and determine where adjustments should be made.

CASEL STANDARDS

- Self-Management

LESSON OUTLINE

INTRODUCTION

Organization is a key element to being successful in most workplaces. However, when you have 20 to 25 students functioning within your workspace every day, organization becomes that much more critical. Not only are you managing your personal space, but you are managing a shared space that students operate in with a seemingly endless amount of papers, writing materials, and books. One of the greatest ways that you can support your students is by providing them with clear systems that can help them stay organized. You also want to be sure that you are acknowledging positive behavior so that it is the standard students strive for every day. Lastly, your personal work time should feel focused and productive so that you are able to get exactly what you need to get done during your cherished prep time.

STRATEGIES

Analyze current systems in your classroom to either keep or change.

If you are in the early years of teaching, classroom systems may be far from your priority at the moment, which is entirely understandable. Systems in the classroom are something that can be developed over many years. For me, changes are often rooted in being asked the same questions so many times that I'm about to lose my cool. For example, my students can't tell time, so I am asked about 30 times a day what time it is. Instead of doing this over and over, I bought a digital clock for students to look at to save myself the sanity. Systems can be as simple as that, or they can be having an absent folder students can go to for any work they missed. Many systems come from a place of wanting to preserve teacher sanity, and when you realize that, you'll probably start to love them.

Determine a positive reinforcement system for your students.

An awesome way to earn buy-in from your students is to establish a positive reinforcement system in your classroom. Personally, I use a strategy called secret student. Every day, I pick a student at random to be the secret student, and throughout class I will narrate whether this secret student is doing a great job or not in class without letting anyone know who it is. At the end of the class, if the student has done well, they earn a prize from my prize binder and I let the class know who the secret student was. If they did not do well, they do not get a prize and the class does not find out who the secret student was that day. I keep a list of my students and check off when they earn the secret student or put an X next to their name if they do not earn it. Once we've been through the whole class, I start fresh with a new list. This system of organization is not overwhelming for me as a teacher, and it helps students stay motivated and excited to learn every day.

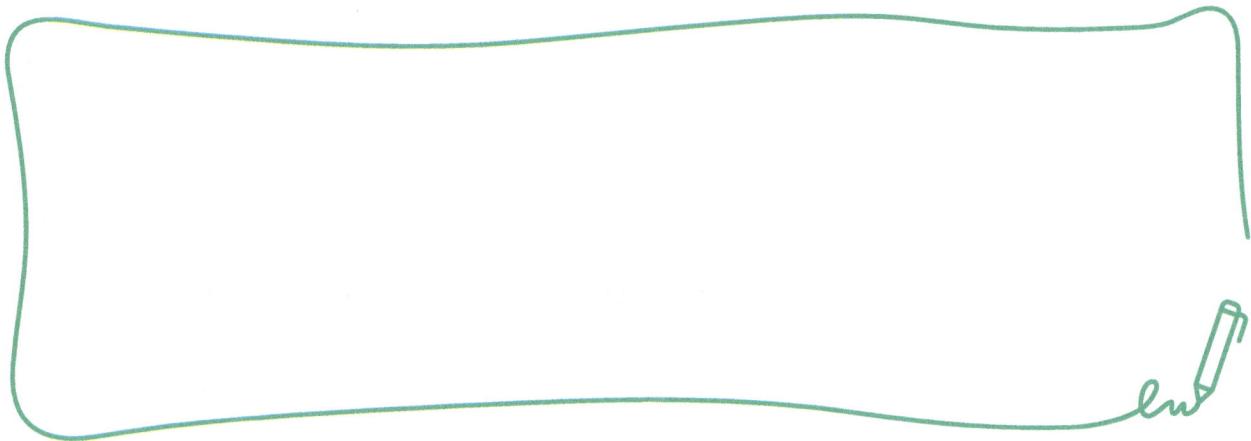

(*Complete Activity 2.*) _____

Assess personal organization system and determine where adjustments should be made.

We've been easing into it, but now it's time to take a look at our personal organization. Do you have a mystery pile toppling over onto your desk? Can you easily find missing work for students when they need it? Are you regularly overwhelmed by your to-do list and unable to get started? Now's our time to iron out these kinks so we can support ourselves in our work as much as we support our students.

ACTIVITIES

Analyze current systems in your classroom to either keep or change.

Below, list any systems you have currently in your classroom. Then, rate them 1-5 in how effective they are. (1 is not at all effective, 5 is it couldn't work better).

Are there any places you could improve these systems that are already in your classroom? How?

Where is there still a need in your classroom for a system? Brainstorm how you can meet this need below.

———————— (Now, complete Reflection 1.) ————————

Determine a positive reinforcement system for your students.

Feel free to also use secret students! Many teachers do and it's a popular way to keep students engaged with low teacher lift. If this doesn't seem right for you, brainstorm a positive reinforcement system for your students below. If you already have one, assess if it is working well, or how you could make this less work for you daily.

_____

_____

_____

———————— (Now, complete Reflection 2.) ————————

Assess personal organization system and determine where adjustments should be made.

_____

_____

_____

In this activity, you will read a word regarding your personal organization and write down the first word that pops into your head about it. Try not to edit your thoughts, just be honest with yourself.

_____

_____

_____

- ◉ Planner
- ◉ Papers
- ◉ Grading System
- ◉ Computer Files
- ◉ Emails
- ◉ Desk Drawers

LESSON PLANS

(Now, complete Reflection 3.)

REFLECTIONS

Reflection 1

- How much room for growth do you have in your classroom systems?

- How can you make your systems the most functional for you AND your students?

◉ Are there any that aren't working? Can you do away with them or improve them somehow?

Reflection 2

◉ How can organizing your positive reinforcement system impact your classroom?

◉ How can you communicate these expectations to your students so that they are clear about how this will work?

◉ Will you need to let families know? If so, how can you easily do so?

Reflection 3

◉ What clear trends did you see in this activity?

⊙   What areas need some reassessing?

⊙   How can you support yourself better in these areas?

PATIENT

(A person who requires medical care)

Educating children can be described as a beautiful struggle. Oftentimes, educationally deprived students refuse to take the medicine of knowledge from teachers. Understandably, teachers grow tired and frustrated of forcing students to partake in something that will be beneficial to them so they retreat to the already healthy students that eagerly wait another heaping of learning to satisfy their hunger for knowledge. Imagine if the classroom was an emergency room and the patients were students in need of extreme "educational" care. Instead of treating "patients" according to who signed in first, the "doctor" would treat them according to their inability to grasp concepts and to understand. Needless to say, the "emergency room" would be less chaotic because the "patients" who are in desperate need of educational attention will be getting the attention they require.

Patient is also defined as "enduring trying circumstances with an even temper." Being a teacher is a difficult challenge to anyone's patience. Students will knowingly and unknowingly frustrate teachers. However, teachers must remain patient even in the most tiring situation and continue to remain confident in their teaching ability. Ralph Marston, an accomplished motivator once stated, "The keys to patience are acceptance and faith. Accept things as they are, and look realistically at the world around you. Have faith in yourself and in the direction you have chosen."

Teachers, in your "emergency room" remain patient to your "patients."

"In time, even grass becomes milk."

Charah Singh"

MENTAL HEALTH LESSON PLAN

Audience: Administrators, Educators, Central Office Personnel & Staff

Subject: Mental Health

Topic: Patient

LESSON GOALS

Explore the idea that, "progress is not linear".

- ○ Consider what you need to do when feeling frustrated or overwhelmed.
- ○ Practice extending grace to yourself and to your students.

CASEL STANDARDS

- ○ Self-Management

LESSON OUTLINE

INTRODUCTION

Oh, patience. We hear the word so often, but always need to be reminded of it more. Regardless of who you are, there are likely moments throughout your day when you need to exercise some more patience. Maybe you need to be patient with yourself after dropping and spilling your coffee. Maybe you need to give that coworker grace who hasn't gotten back to you about the student you're worried about. Or maybe, it's the student who once again refuses to pick up his pencil and get to work. There are very few situations where getting upset and frustrated with yourself or others can actually help resolve the issue you are facing. However, if you take a deep breath, take a moment to center yourself, and attempt to act rationally, you will be on a much better path.

STRATEGIES

Explore the idea that, "progress is not linear".

Have you ever heard of the phrase, "progress is not linear"? This means that some moments are just going to feel hard sometimes. Even if you've had a student who was finally participating more and more in class, there may be a day when she comes in and it feels like you're back at square one again. However, remaining patient with her will help her get back on track. We have to remember that progress is not linear with others, and also not with ourselves. Sometimes a situation is less than ideal, but it's how we respond with consistency and patience that can lead to the best outcome.

Consider what you need to do when feeling frustrated or overwhelmed.

In order to be your best, most patient self, it is important to take care of yourself. A way to care for yourself is to prepare for a moment where you may feel upset or overwhelmed, and consider how you can help yourself make a good choice in that moment. For instance instead of blurting something out at a coworker when you are frustrated, perhaps instead you can take a deep breath, and write out a note in your phone expressing how you feel that you can look back at when you feel more centered. This way, you aren't making your feelings anyone else's problem, and are exercising a healthy amount of patience with that person and with yourself.

_____ (Complete Activity 2.) _____

Practice extending grace to yourself and to your students.

In theory, it's easy to say what the right thing is to do in stressful situations. However, truly acting from a place of patience each time a challenging situation comes up is a different story. We are going to practice responding to some different stressful situations in the following activity.

ACTIVITIES

Explore the idea that, "progress is not linear".

Think about a time in your personal life where progress hasn't been linear.

In the space below, sketch how the progress looked. Label the peaks and the pits as you go. It should look a bit like a heart monitor.

Now, think about a student whose progress you've been keeping track of lately. Think about where your student could eventually end up if you remain consistent. Sketch what this may look like below.

———————————— *(Now, complete Reflection 1.)* ————————————

Consider what you need to do when feeling frustrated or overwhelmed.

What do you need when you feel upset or overwhelmed? List three things you can do in the moment to calm yourself down, even while teaching in the classroom.

You can also make these moments teaching moments for your students! How can you practice this coping strategy and also teach it to your students? For example, I feel overwhelmed and jumbled. It helps me to listen to a meditation when I feel this way, so I put on a meditation for the entire class to benefit from a moment of mindfulness.

_____ (Now, complete Reflection 2.) _____

Practice extending grace to yourself and to your students.

Read the following situations. After each one, close your eyes, take a deep breath, and type out how you could patiently respond.

Your student pulls out the chair from under another student, and the student who was trying to sit down falls on the ground.

Your principal sent you an email observation full of critiques about your lesson, but you had everything planned out intentionally, which he couldn't see from the short period of time he saw your class.

The same student who has asked you 35 questions already in class has her hand up again.

_____ (Now, complete Reflection 3.) _____

REFLECTIONS

Reflection 1

◉   When a student falls short on making progress, what is commonly your reaction?

◉ How can you reframe this so that you can be more patient with the progress?

◉ When progress starts to feel like it is going backward with a student, what can you do to help yourself and the student stay on track?

Reflection 2

◉ How can you remind yourself of your strategies in a moment of stress?

◉ Do you need anything to support you in moments where you are exercising patience? For example, a coworker to step in while you take a quick walk to reset.

◉ Why would sharing this moment of reset be beneficial for your students?

Reflection 3

- ◉ Why did we have you take a moment of pause?

_____

_____

_____

- ◉ How often do you give yourself that moment of pause before responding?

_____

_____

_____

- ◉ How can thinking through likely situations ahead of time help you feel prepared for them to happen in real life?

_____

_____

_____

QUALITY

(A degree or grade of excellence or worth)

William Foster, United States Marine who received a Medal of Honor said, "Quality is never an accident; it is always the result of high intention, sincere effort, intelligent direction and skillful execution; it represents the wise choice of many alternatives." You didn't just happen to stumble in a classroom. You are in a classroom because you willed yourself in that direction. In college, you had the ambition to wake up every morning for four or more years and attend dozens of classes with demanding professors as the host. Most of you had jobs but still forced yourself to study for exams after long stressful days of serving others. Some of you had families you had to cater to but you still managed to complete a bachelor's, master's and advanced degrees in your field. However, you still conquered obstacles that were placed in your way by the university and you completed all the necessary requirements to become a teacher in Mississippi. You have proven to others, but more importantly to yourself, that you represent the highest degree of excellence. You are quality so you must demand and accept no less from your students.

Demand quality and you will receive it.

MENTAL HEALTH LESSON PLAN

Audience: Administrators, Educators, Central Office Personnel & Staff   **Subject:** Mental Health   **Topic:** Quality

LESSON GOALS

Determine what quality looks like as an educator.

- ○ Brainstorm what determines quality in your students' behavior.
- ○ Learn to balance quality with realistic expectations.

CASEL STANDARDS

- ○ Self-Awareness

LESSON OUTLINE

INTRODUCTION

The quality that we expect in our work, whether that is the expectations we place on ourselves or the expectations we place on our students, is deeply important to consider. If you are not showing up with a passion for teaching, enthusiasm for the job, and endless encouragement for your students, they're not likely reciprocating with their best effort. When you show up as your best self, students feel empowered to show up as their best selves. Of course it's a two-way street, and what you expect from your students about the quality of their work communicates your level of belief in them. If your expectations for your students are low, their motivation to reach those expectations will also be low. However, if you set the bar at an appropriate level, students will feel motivated and empowered to reach it because they can feel your belief in them. In this lesson, we will talk about how you hold yourself accountable to quality work, as well as how you hold your students accountable. Lastly, we will consider how these high expectations can be reached realistically without causing teacher burnout and excessive student stress.

STRATEGIES

Determine what quality looks like as an educator.

What would the ideal educator be like? What would they do? Say? How would they act? How do they bring quality to each lesson, interaction, and piece of feedback? Yes, likely a lot of coffee is involved. But also, someone simply cannot bring an impressive quality to work in the classroom without investing in themselves first. We can't pour from an empty cup, and we can not expect our students to thrive when we, arguably their most influential role models, are struggling ourselves.

_____ (Now, complete Activity 1.) _____

Brainstorm what determines quality in your students' behavior.

Just as one would envision their ideal self to become it, we should also envision our ideal class to help it come to life. Just as we can't hold unrealistic expectations for ourselves, we can't hold unrealistic expectations for others. However, in general, we know what we hope to see in the classroom.

_____ (Complete Activity 2.) _____

Learn to balance quality with realistic expectations.

Often, teachers are asked to do the impossible. We juggle countless tasks, answer a million questions a day, and are emotionally invested in our work. However, there will be days where we fall flat. There will be days when our students disappoint us. It's okay if we fall, but what matters is that we always get up.

_____ *(Now, complete Activity 3.)* _____

ACTIVITIES

Determine what quality looks like as an educator.

In the left column, make a list of the things you would expect to see from a high quality educator. Then on the right, list how you think they are able to deliver that level of quality.

_____ *(Now, complete Reflection 1.)* _____

Brainstorm what determines quality in your students' behavior.

In your ideal classroom, what do you hope to be true about your students' behavior?

What do you hope to be true about the work that they produce?

———————— (Now, complete Reflection 2.) ————————

Learn to balance quality with realistic expectations.

Write yourself a letter (about a paragraph in length) for a hard teaching day. Talk to yourself as you would your best friend.

_____

_____

_____

Now, write your student a letter for a day that they are struggling. Approach them with grace, care, and encouragement.

_____

_____

_____

———————— (Now, complete Reflection 3.) ————————

REFLECTIONS

Reflection 1

- In what areas are you already doing high quality work?

_____

_____

- Where is there room to grow?

_____

_____

- How can you ensure that your self care is supporting you in this work?

_____

_____

Reflection 2

- How can you model what you'd like to see in your students in your own behavior?

- How can you scaffold for students so they can reach this bar of success?

- How can you prepare yourself for moments where students are not reaching your expectations, and respond with grace and empathy?

Reflection 3

- How did it feel writing yourself this letter?

- Do you find yourself speaking to your students in a similar way to what you wrote in your letter to them?

- How can you move forward holding this compassion for yourself and your students, while still holding a standard of high quality?

R

RECEPTIVE

(Open to arguments, ideas, or change)

Receptive teachers understand that they must be open-minded;—able to adjust to the various needs by students. They understand that they must seek unbiased feedback from their audience and alter their teaching approach. That will be of great benefit to their students. Teaching is a lot like the medical profession or law because it's a practice. Educational framework is constantly changing through local, state and national legislation. From *Bloom's Taxonomy* to *Webb's Depth of Knowledge* someone's thoughts on how to properly educate children will always be on the forefront of teaching a class. As teachers, we must be receptive to these ideas but more importantly we must listen to our students and accommodate their needs.

I worked within a community college and university setting for a total of three years and at the end of every course students had to complete a survey listing the professor's strengths and weaknesses; areas of effectiveness and areas of non-effectiveness; and suggest ways the instructor could improve instruction. I think this method could be highly effective in the K-12 setting because teachers will be receiving unfiltered feedback directly from their students. Once the teacher receives the feedback they can improve their teaching approach and reach more students.

MENTAL HEALTH LESSON PLAN

Audience: Administrators, Educators, Central Office Personnel & Staff   **Subject:** Mental Health   **Topic:** Receptive

LESSON GOALS

Determine the importance of regularly reassessing teaching approaches.

- ○ Identify the benefits of collecting feedback.
- ○ Practice accommodating practices to feedback.

CASEL STANDARDS

- ○ Self-Awareness

LESSON OUTLINE

INTRODUCTION

Teaching is called a practice because it will never be perfect. It can, however, always be improved and revised. Every day people are coming out with new research and practices that can better support our students and as responsive teachers, it is our duty to respond to those changes and reflect them in our classroom. Regardless of how many years we've been teaching, it can always be of value to incorporate new learnings into your craft. Similar to how a product would get reviews from their consumers, our students are our consumers and their feedback matters. You may think you gave a lesson that was extremely engaging and thought provoking, but your students may have actually gotten very little out of it. Receptive teachers are always open to hearing the feedback of their students and using that feedback to better their teaching practices in the future. We want our students to be sponges taking in all of the information that they learn and using it to make better choices tomorrow. In a similar way, we have to practice what we preach and commit to being better teachers every day for our students.

STRATEGIES

Determine the importance of regularly reassessing teaching approaches.

One of the beautiful and challenging things about working in the education field is that people will consistently come up with newer and better ways to help students learn academic content. Just as we wouldn't want our doctor to be outdated in the science that she is using in order to perform surgery, we don't want a teacher to be relying on older practices either. In order to best serve our students, we must adapt to current research and use these new findings in our classroom.

(Now, complete Activity 1.)

Identify the benefits of collecting feedback.

Since young people aren't necessarily as intelligent as adults, their opinions are often hushed by the opinions of adults. However, why would we ask a human how tasty dog food is? Why would we ask a toddler if a wheelchair was designed well? Of course these are extreme examples, but you get the idea. In order to know how to best teach kids, you have to ask them because they're the ones learning. Some responses may be silly and some may be vague, but young people can always surprise you with their candor.

(Complete Activity 2.)

Practice accommodating practices to feedback.

Receiving and reading the feedback is part 1. Now, you need to do the work that really matters, which is to use this feedback to better your teaching practice. If this feels overwhelming to you at first, start small. Save all of the helpful responses in a bank, and look at them one at a time. Looking at your upcoming week's lesson plan, how can you incorporate more of what your student suggested into it? Do you believe that doing so will improve your teaching practice?

(Now, complete Activity 3.)

ACTIVITIES

1. **Determine the importance of regularly reassessing teaching approaches.**

   Take a moment to reflect below.

How often do you consider the ways in which you can teach a certain topic?

Are you in the loop with any like-minded education groups that share recent findings in the field?

If not, how can we connect to some educators like yourself who are committed to incorporating current findings into their practice?

(Now, complete Reflection 1.)

2. **Identify the benefits of collecting feedback.**

Below, list some possible benefits of collecting feedback from your students. List at least 8. Try to push yourself, and try to commit to that number.

_____ (Now, complete Reflection 2.) _____

3. **Practice accommodating practices to feedback.**

Read the following pieces of feedback. Then, think about how you could go about incorporating that into your upcoming week's lessons.

"We sit a lot in math class. I think I would have an easier time focusing if we moved around more."

_____

_____

"We take so many notes, and I know that I don't learn best by writing every word down. Can there be more options for kids like me?"

_____

_____

"Sometimes you read everything in class, and it can get boring to listen to. I think it would be nice to hear other people's voices, too."

_____

_____

_____ (Now, complete Reflection 3.) _____

REFLECTIONS

Reflection 1

- ◉ Why is it important to regularly adapt our teaching methods?

_____

_____

- ◉ What are the dangers of not adapting our teaching practices?

_____

_____

◉ What are the benefits of doing so regularly?

Reflection 2

◉ What did you realize from this activity?

◉ Did anything surprise you?

◉ How could you incorporate feedback into your teaching regularly?

Reflection 3

◉ What did these suggestions make you wonder?

◉ How does thinking this through change your practice moving forward?

◉ How can you keep this feedback in a place you can refer back to when you are reviewing your pedagogical practices?

SMART

(Showing mental alertness and calculation and resourcefulness)

Being smart doesn't necessarily have to mean a person maintained a 4.0 average throughout school, but it does mean that the person understood what had to be done in order to progress to the next level. Smart teachers located in the Mississippi Delta and in the lands abroad understand being mentally alert. They know to establish a high level of excellence during the first day of class and to maintain excellence throughout the school year. Smart teachers know they must be calculating, planning lessons that will challenge the most mentally talented student. They know that whispering gossip behind closed doors will not get them the resources they need so instead they write letters to stakeholders, they petition local businesses for tangible aid and they cheerfully go to work everyday knowing they are facing a grueling challenge.

MENTAL HEALTH LESSON PLAN

Audience: Administrators, Educators, Central Office Personnel & Staff   **Subject:** Mental Health   **Topic:** Smart

LESSON GOALS

Reflect on the mental alertness required to be an effective educator.

- ○ Determine the calculations necessary to ensure student growth.
- ○ Identify what resources you can utilize to foster the best learning environment possible.

CASEL STANDARDS

- ○ Self-Awareness

LESSON OUTLINE

INTRODUCTION

The old saying, "If you can't... teach," is outdated and laughable. Effective teachers need to be incredibly smart people, who constantly think on their feet. They are always juggling managing materials and student behaviors, while aiming to drive a lesson forward that is engaging, challenging, and can prove mastery. Every day they are collecting data, planning effective delivery of content, and managing family emotions about their students' behavior. First, we need to acknowledge that what teachers do every day is superhuman. Then, we can put this brilliance to good use to think about how we can hone our skills more intentionally to determine how our students can make more growth. Lastly, we will consider what research we can do when we don't know what the best practice is, and where we can go to find this information.

STRATEGIES

Reflect on the mental alertness required to be an effective educator.

If you are a teacher, this part does not need to be taught to you. Acknowledge the many, many things that you do in your role as "teacher" every day. Think in particular about the things outside of actually teaching. However, for a change, you don't have to do anything about them right now. We're just going to reflect on them.

———————————— *(Now, complete Activity 1.)* ————————————

Determine the calculations necessary to ensure student growth.

Next we are going to do a deeper dive on your student data. Depending on your subject that you teach, you are likely looking at a list of objectives that you need your students to master this year in order to be ready to move on to next year. You will consider how you collect your student data currently, and if this is giving you a clear picture of whether or not your students are on track.

———————————————————————————

———————————————————————————

———————————— *(Complete Activity 2.)* ————————————

Identify what resources you can utilize to foster the best learning environment possible.

Although you are amazing, there is likely an educator out there that has more experience, has done more research, or is simply more of an expert in a certain realm than you are. Luckily, this isn't a competition. If people have shared this information publicly, it's yours to tap into! Consider some places in your content area where you know you could get a better understanding of the material yourself. If you feel truly solid in all areas, how could you think about teaching this material in a way that is better for students? This is where your work lies!

———————————————————————————

———————————————————————————

———————————— *(Now, complete Activity 3.)* ————————————

ACTIVITIES

In the space below, draw a stick figure, the best that you can, juggling. This person is juggling all of the many things that you have to juggle throughout your work day. Go ahead and label those things - as many as you can think of.

———————————————————————————

———————————————————————————

———————————————————————————

Determine the calculations necessary to ensure student growth.

Do you have a current strategy for measuring your students' formative growth? Summative growth? If you need more of one or the other, how do you see yourself incorporating more of this into your teaching?

_____

_____

_____

How are you yourself recording this data, so you can use it to plan for future teaching? If you don't already have a method, how can you develop one?

_____

_____

_____

_____ (Now, complete Reflection 2.) _____

Identify what resources you can utilize to foster the best learning environment possible.

What do you currently refer to when you need some guidance on teaching material?

_____

_____

_____

Where are the other places you can look that you aren't utilizing? Try to name at least 5. (I promise, there are at LEAST 5!)

_____

_____

_____

REFLECTIONS

Reflection 1

◉ Why is it important to acknowledge all that you do throughout the school day?

◉ What skills do this level of "juggling" require?

◉ How can you give yourself more credit for all that you do on your more difficult teaching days?

Reflection 2

◉ Why is data collection so crucial to student success?

◉ How is formative data helpful while looking at student growth?

◉ How is summative data helpful while looking at student growth?

Reflection 3

- On a scale of 1-5 how would you rate yourself in using the wealth of knowledge that's available to you?

- How can you commit to using more of that knowledge?

- Why will this be beneficial to your students?

TRUSTWORTHY

(Worthy of trust or belief)

In most cases, young students and teenagers equate success with the way they feel towards a particular teacher. If a student feels that the teacher has violated or will violate his best interest then he will not put his best effort forward in that class. As "silly" as that sounds it's very true. The same is true for an administrator who has violated a teacher's trust by spreading gossip or partaking in acts unbecoming of a professional. Children often become involved in relationships with other children only to have their secrets aired to the public, thus making them feel violated and unable to express their true feelings to people. Thomas Moore, arguably one of the world's greatest poets, once said, "We need people in our lives with whom we can be as open as possible. To have real conversation with people may seem like such a simple, obvious suggestion, but it involves courage and risk." Principals, counselors and teachers must recognize that students are taking risks by opening up and expressing themselves. Adults must remain professional enough not to disclose secrets because if a student suspects you have done otherwise the student will never treat you the same again.

When someone trust you they feel comfortable around you; if they feel comfortable around they will be more receptive to your teachings.

MENTAL HEALTH LESSON PLAN

Audience: Administrators, Educators, Central Office Personnel & Staff   **Subject:** Mental Health   **Topic:** Trustworthy

LESSON GOALS

Reflect on adults you've trusted or not trusted in your youth.

- Establish the importance of gaining student trust.
- Learn how to affirm student vulnerability and openness.

CASEL STANDARDS

- Self-Awareness

LESSON OUTLINE

INTRODUCTION

Everyone learns best when they are in an environment that they feel safe in. Safety is largely centered around trust. If you establish a learning space where students know that they can ask questions, make mistakes, and trust you to help them when they need it, you are doing an important role as their teacher. Many students don't have an adult in their lives that they can truly trust, so it is imperative that you, as their teacher, are being that safe adult for them.

STRATEGIES

Reflect on adults you've trusted or not trusted in your youth.

First, you will reflect on the adults that were in your life when you were younger. Did you have any teachers that felt safe to go to if you were struggling personally? If you had a question about the learning materials? Or did you have teachers who would shame you if you did anything wrong, make you feel stupid when you didn't get a question right, and who overall, made you feel anxious in their learning space?

———————————— *(Now, complete Activity 1.)* ————————————

Establish the importance of gaining student trust.

Next we are going to think more deeply about why it is important for a teacher to be trustworthy. In many cases, school makes young people anxious. Some students feel like they are in fight or flight mode when they are in the classroom, because the stressors of school feel like too much. When students are in this panicked, high strung state, it makes it very difficult for them to learn. Therefore, by getting to know students better, accommodating to their individual needs, and becoming a person they know they can go to for help will allow them to feel more safe and able to grasp new concepts.

———————————— *(Complete Activity 2.)* ————————————

Learn how to affirm student vulnerability and openness.

A very important way to gain student trust is to affirm their vulnerability. When a student who doesn't usually ask questions advocates for help, make sure you tell them that you are proud of them for that! When a student shares something personal about themselves, be sure to thank them. We never want students to feel ashamed when they open up to us, because through asking questions and working through their thought processes, this is where the learning happens.

———————————— *(Now, complete Activity 3.)* ————————————

ACTIVITIES

1. **Reflect on adults you've trusted or not trusted in your youth.**

List five teachers you had when you were younger. Then, identify them with an "s" for safe, and a "u" for unsafe. Lastly, list three reasons you labeled each teacher either as safe or unsafe. For example: Ms. Phelps was safe because she always did what she said she was going to do.

_____

_____

_____

_____

_____ (Now, complete Reflection 1.) _____

Establish the importance of gaining student trust.

Reflect: When you trust someone, how does it benefit your relationship when you are together?

When a student trusts you, how do you think it will benefit your teacher-student relationship?

_____ (Now, complete Reflection 2.) _____

2. **Learn how to affirm student vulnerability and openness.**

For the following situations, respond with affirmation of the student's vulnerability.

Your student just shared with you that their pet is sick, and that they're very worried about it.

_____

_____

_____

Your student asked you a question during a test.

_____

_____

_____

Your student who doesn't usually raise his hand did, and asked a question in class.

_____

_____

_____

_____ *(Now, complete Reflection 3.)* _____

REFLECTIONS

Reflection 1

◉ What was a takeaway from this activity?

_____

_____

◉ Did any teachers make you feel safe by doing something that you can incorporate more into your teaching?

_____

_____

◉ Did any teachers make you feel unsafe by doing something that you sometimes do?

Reflection 2

◉ Why does trust matter in relationships?

◉ What stressors did you juggle at school?

◉ How could a teacher that you trusted have helped with some of these stressors?

Reflection 3

◉ Why can affirmation be powerful?

◉ How do you feel when someone affirms you when you are vulnerable?

◉ Which student would you like to be more intentional about affirming in your classroom?

UPBEAT

(Pleasant and optimistic)

Overbearing administrators, getting paid once a month, lack of parental and community involvement, behavioral problems, disenchanted students and lengthy after-school meetings are only a few items that compose a long list of reasons why teachers can be troubled. Teachers have every right to be angry—even pessimistic. However, you cannot succumb to the simple trappings of harboring negative attitudes towards life's offerings. Anger isn't necessarily a bad emotion to express in a classroom. For an example, if a teacher has thoroughly taught an objective only to have the majority of students fail the exam then the teacher should express disappointment. However, despite the failing test scores and other negative distracters try to keep a pleasant personality and an optimistic attitude because you have the ability to change the situation simply by changing your attitude about it. Mary Engelbreit, author and positive thinking guru, acknowledged, **"If you don't like something, change it; if you can't change it, change the way you think about it."** If you apply this simple concept within your workplace you will not have a problem at maintaining an upbeat attitude.

REINHOLD NIEBUHR'S SERENITY PRAYER

God grant me the serenity

To accept the things I cannot change;

Courage to change the things I can;

And wisdom to know the difference.

You have worked very hard to become an educator. Be proud of your accomplishments. Don't let a child, parent or administrator alter your optimistic mood.

MENTAL HEALTH LESSON PLAN

Audience: Administrators, Educators, Central Office Personnel & Staff **Subject:** Mental Health **Topic:** Upbeat

LESSON GOALS

Practice the power of gratitude.

- Brainstorm what is and is not in your locus of control.
- Create a system for saving joyful moments to return back to.

CASEL STANDARDS

- Self Management

LESSON OUTLINE

INTRODUCTION

Some days, being a teacher can feel like an uphill battle. There's always a student who needs your attention, a parent hoping for a meeting, papers to grade, emails to answer, better practices to incorporate, and tomorrow's lessons to plan. With all that being said, you set the tone for your classroom space. If you feel overwhelmed, negative, and pessimistic, that's how your students will feel in your classroom too. However, if you set the space up with vibrant energy, positivity, and grace, your learners will feel that energy and reflect it back to you. Not to mention, you'll like your job a lot more.

STRATEGIES

Practice the power of gratitude.

Research continues to show that practicing gratitude is one of the most powerful ways to increase our happiness and contentment. It can feel easy to get bogged down in the overwhelm of the work day, but be mindful about what things you are also grateful for.

———————— *(Now, complete Activity 1.)* ————————

Brainstorm what is and is not in your locus of control.

Often teachers are perfectionists. We work hard, do our jobs well, and care deeply for our students. A key part of being a teacher and avoiding burnout is understanding what is and is not in your control. Although we want to be able to do everything to support our students, sometimes we need to focus on our role, and simply teach.

———————— *(Complete Activity 2.)* ————————

Create a system for saving joyful moments to return back to.

Reminding yourself of moments that make your job special is so important on our hard days. Do not let a moment of gratitude slip away without you capturing it somewhere you can refer back to later. One of my favorite things I do is keep a record of hilarious or sweet things that my students say. When I'm feeling down or unmotivated, I go back and reread those quotes, and immediately my outlook shifts to feeling fortunate I get to work with young people the way that I do.

———————— *(Now, complete Activity 3.)* ————————

ACTIVITIES

Practice the power of gratitude.

For the next week, take a moment once your students leave the classroom to write three things you are grateful for that happened that day. Each day, also read what you wrote the previous day.

| Monday |
| Tuesday |
| Wednesday |
| Thursday |
| Friday |

1. **Brainstorm what is and is not in your locus of control.**

   ⦿ Read the following prayer.

   ⦿ God grant me the serenity

   ⦿ To accept the things I cannot change;

   ⦿ Courage to change the things I can;

   ⦿ And wisdom to know the difference.

   ⦿ What are some of the things you feel the responsibility to change, but know that you cannot?

2. **How does this impact you and your work?**

Create a system for saving joyful moments to return back to.

What's your favorite way to remember special moments? Do you like to write it down, keep a note on your phone, or snap a picture? Decide a way that you will remember these special moments, and commit to returning to them when you are having a hard moment.

REFLECTIONS

Reflection 1

◉ How did you feel before and after your gratitude practice?

◉ Did you notice a shift in your overall mood throughout the week?

◉ What was it like looking back at the previous day, even when you were tired at the end of the day you just had?

Reflection 2

◉ What do you have control over in your classroom?

◉ How often do things out of your locus of control feel like your responsibility?

◉ What's a way you can remind yourself of the difference?

Reflection 3

◉ Have you ever noticed how negative comments seem to stick around longer than positive ones? How can keeping track of the positive moments help you stay more upbeat at work?

◉ What's your favorite thing a student has said to you?

◉ If you don't keep track of nice things your coworkers or bosses say to you, consider doing this too! How could you record these things?

VISIONARY

(A person given to fanciful speculations and enthusiasms with little regard for what is actually possible.)

If you have taught for more than a few years you have observed the dramatic changes students go through at various points in their life. Students you thought weren't going to college because they weren't "smart enough" actually went and excelled, becoming productive model citizens. Teachers must have the foresight to see children as what they can become with guidance from a supportive and encouraging teacher. Visionary teachers understand that there are no limitations within the classroom's walls and that anything is possible with faith, hard work and detailed planning. Yolanda Devers, a three time Olympic champion who battled Graves' disease, once stated, "Keep your dreams alive. Understand to achieve anything requires faith and belief in yourself, vision, hard work, determination, and dedication. Remember all things are possible for those who believe." Well in advance, effective teachers ask themselves, "How can I maximize my students' success and diligently maneuver them from where they are to where they need to be?"

Christopher Columbus had an extremely difficult time obtaining permission from the European governments to explore the Unknown. Time after time again Columbus went asking for permission only to be denied. However, the vision Columbus had of the "New World" was far more powerful than the word "no." In your classrooms, you must have the vision of Columbus: To look over the vastness of a void ocean and see something no one else can see and to let that vision drive and motivate you into something the world has never before seen.

Believe in your success; in yourself...believe in your visions.

MENTAL HEALTH LESSON PLAN

Audience: Administrators, Educators, Central Office Personnel & Staff   **Subject:** Mental Health   **Topic:** Visionary

LESSON GOALS

Describe your highest teacher self.

- ○ Visualize a bright future for a student of yours who is struggling.
- ○ Practice giving a pep talk to that student.

CASEL STANDARDS

- ○ Self-Awareness

LESSON OUTLINE

INTRODUCTION

Teachers are inherently hopeful visionaries. The reason we do the work that we do is because we can see the bright futures of our students, and believe that the work that we do with them every day will help them get there. If we believe that our students will become their most fulfilled selves, our students will feel that every day, and hopefully, believe it as well.

STRATEGIES

Write out your highest teacher self.

First, we are going to look inward. You have to believe in your own power before convincing someone else of theirs. Think about who you are as an educator, and who you, as your most fulfilled, and best self, is as an educator. Once we consider this version of ourselves, it is easier to act in alignment with the person we hope to become.

———————— (Now, complete Activity 1.) ————————

Visualize a bright future for a student of yours who is struggling.

Students see right through inauthenticity. If it is clear that you do not believe what you are saying yourself, your students won't buy it. Therefore, it can be a very powerful exercise to visualize your students as their highest selves, and begin to really believe that you are a key component in helping them get there.

———————— (Complete Activity 2.) ————————

Practice giving a pep talk to a student.

Now is where this work becomes concrete. We've all been the teacher who is desperately trying to encourage a student who is disengaged, overwhelmed, or upset. We are going to practice giving this student a pep talk, thinking about the person we believe they can become, and helping them believe they can and will be that person someday, and that their choices in this moment can help them get there.

———————— (Now, complete Activity 3.) ————————

ACTIVITIES

1. **Write out your highest teacher self.**

In the space below, brainstorm your most wonderful ideal version of yourself as an educator. What kinds of things do you say? What do you do? How does your classroom feel?

_____

_____

_____

_____

Now, try not to be too hard on yourself. Go back through and circle the things you already know that you embody in your teaching practice. It may not be every minute of every day, but think generally.

—————————— (Now, complete Reflection 1.) ——————————

2. **Visualize a bright future for a student of yours who is struggling.**

Pick a student of yours who you know is having a difficult time in the classroom. List below what you know about them and what they hope to become some day.

_____

_____

_____

_____

Now, close your eyes, and imagine you are a fly on the wall in their most beautiful, fully fulfilled adult life. You feel pride swell in your chest as you see how joyful they are. You smile realizing that your presence and guidance helped them get there.

_____

_____

_____

_____

—————————— (Now, complete Reflection 2.) ——————————

3. **Practice giving a pep talk to that student.**

Think of the same student you visualized in the last exercise. Now think of a struggle this student often faces, and imagine you are observing your student in that struggle in front of you. It's your job to pick them up. What could you say to them?

_____

_____

_____

_____

REFLECTIONS

Reflection 1

◉   How did this activity feel for you?

◉   What kind of encouragement could have helped you in this process?

◉   How could you encourage your students to envision their highest selves?

Reflection 2

◉   How did this exercise impact you?

◉ How could visualizing your students like this affect your teaching?

◉ What do they need to believe about themselves to get to this place?

Reflection 3

◉ How often do you have moments of encouragement like this with your students?

◉ Even if your student doesn't respond at the moment, how could this impact them?

◉ Do you remember someone giving you a pep talk like this?

WISE

(Judicious; marked by the exercise of good judgment or common sense in practical matters.)

Let's not confuse smart with wise. A smart person has mental alertness and has the ability to effectively use resources that may be available to him or her. A wise person has the ability to use high-quality judgment to resolve the most challenging situations in practical ways. For an example, if two children were about to get into an altercation that could result in suspension or worst then a wise teacher would address the two of them to identify the problem. After identifying the problem a wise teacher would suggest alternative methods of solving it instead of fighting. It may seem simple, but it's not. A wise teacher knows the importance of the tone of voice, facial expressions and to confront the issue in private instead in the openness of a classroom. Robert Ingersoll once stated, "It is a thousand times better to have common sense without education than to have education without common sense." However if you combine education with common sense then you will be an unstoppable force. Wise teachers:

1. Know that every child can be highly successful.
2. Understand the importance of time and not to waste it arguing with students.
3. Understand that problems will arise in a classroom setting.
4. Know to change teaching methods if too many children are failing.
5. Know to model behavior of excellence if they wish to see it within their classroom.

MENTAL HEALTH LESSON PLAN

Audience: Administrators, Educators, Central Office Personnel & Staff   **Subject:** Mental Health   **Topic:** Wise

LESSON GOALS

Practice a perspective check.

- ○ Acknowledge your power in the classroom space.
- ○ Be open to being wrong.

CASEL STANDARDS

- ○ Responsible Decision Making

LESSON OUTLINE

INTRODUCTION

Wisdom comes with time. As a first year teacher, the classroom can feel like constant chaos, and every move may feel like impulse. But over time, your responses soften, they become more thoughtful, and you are able to navigate the classroom dynamics with more ease and strategy. Although sometimes teaching can feel like constantly being on your toes, taking a moment to step back and realize the power your presence has in the classroom can always help you get back to a centered place.

STRATEGIES

Practice a perspective check.

When your students are repeatedly ignoring your directions, yelling over each other, and being disrespectful, it can feel easy to want to respond with a yell... or a sarcastic, nasty comment...or with the sharp frustration you feel in your chest. But in these moments, it is important to take a step back, and return to your center.

Now, complete Activity 1.)

Acknowledge your power in the classroom space.

What we often forget as teachers is the power that we hold in our classroom. Some days it may feel like the class walks in, and you have to catch up or come down to their energy, but in reality, they are looking to you. You set the tone for your space, and when you move with calmness and kindness, so will they.

(Complete Activity 2.)

Be open to being wrong.

Truly wise teachers realize that they are never done learning. Even the best, most honored teachers will still say or do things that they shouldn't sometimes. It's okay to still be human and make mistakes. What's more important is that we are careful not to beat ourselves up when we make these mistakes, but to realize that teaching is incredibly hard, and we are doing a remarkably difficult and incredible thing every day. It is okay and it is important to still be growing.

(Now, complete Activity 3.)

ACTIVITIES

1. **Practice a perspective check.**

Think back to the most out of control moment of teaching you've had. Maybe it took you all class to try to get a word in about the lesson. Maybe students were all over the room, ignoring your directions. Think about the panic and the lack of control you felt in this moment. Now, put your hand on your chest and take a deep breath. Remember that your students are safe. Remember that you are safe. Take another deep breath. Now, take a moment to assess the situation, and respond instead of react.

2. **Acknowledge your power in the classroom space.**

Below, list some ways that you can positively alter the energy in your room.

Are there any shifts in your behavior?

Shifts in the physical room?

Shifts in what students see or hear?

——————— (Now, complete Reflection 2.) ———————

3. Be open to being wrong.

Now is when you get to give yourself a pep talk. Imagine you just snapped back at a student after they asked you (once again) for help on the same problem you've already explained to them 5 times. Instead of beating yourself up about this, think about what you can say to yourself to show yourself grace in your weak moment.

——————— (Now, complete Reflection 3.) ———————

REFLECTIONS

Reflection 1

◉   How often do you take a step back in moments of overwhelm?

◉   How effective are you in those panicky states?

◉   How can you remind yourself to have a perspective shift in these moments?

Reflection 2

- Are these shifts feasible for you to work toward?

- What is the first one that you will try, and how do you think it will impact your space?

- What's it like to know your influence on your students?

Reflection 3

- How likely are you to admit that you are wrong?

- Why is acknowledging your humanness so important to being a good teacher?

- Could you do this in front of your students? How might it impact them?

X

XENIAL

(Hospitable, especially to visitors)

1 Peter 4:8-9 states, "Above all, love each other deeply, because love covers over a multitude of sins. Offer hospitality to one another without grumbling." When students enter your classroom they are visiting guest. You are charged with the responsibility of not only making them efficient learners but you hold the task of being respectful and hospitable. When I was teaching in the 7-12 setting, teachers had to stand outside the door and greet students as they entered the classrooms. *Most* times when a child entered, I smiled and said the appropriate greeting such as, "Good Morning" or "Good Afternoon" even if I didn't feel like seeing a particular child. I tried my best to make them feel comfortable while they were in my classroom.

How would you feel if you asked someone for a favor; they agreed, but the entire time they performed the favor they complained and grumbled in your presence? If you're anything like me, their behavior would probably make you regret asking them for anything. The same is true for the students we teach. We can't greet them with a smiling face only to complain that they are present. A proverb suggests, "It is a sin against hospitality, to open your doors and darken your countenance." Greet them and remain fond of your guest; they are only visiting and the bell will sound before you know it.

MENTAL HEALTH LESSON PLAN

Audience: Administrators, Educators, Central Office Personnel & Staff   **Subject:** Mental Health   **Topic:** Xenial

LESSON GOALS

Describe the most xenial classroom you can imagine.

- Consider how to offer hospitality in your classroom.
- Reflect on the classroom spaces you grew up in.

CASEL STANDARDS

- Relationship Skills

LESSON OUTLINE

INTRODUCTION

When we consider inviting guests into our home, we are always thinking about how we can impress them. We do a deep clean, we put out nice flowers, and do everything we can to ensure that our guests feel invited and welcomed into our home. Twenty-something students come into our classroom every day, which sometimes makes the classroom space feel dominated by them, their energies, and their materials. However, if we shift that narrative, we can explore the idea that students are guests in the classroom space, and we need to do what we can to best serve them while they're there.

STRATEGIES

Describe the most xenial classroom you can imagine.

There are many things that we can do to help students feel successful in the classroom space. It can start at their entrance, where you give them a warm greeting. You can make the learning space tidy and free of clutter, so their focus can be on learning. There can be things for them to look at that inspire, uplift, and motivate them to show up as their best selves. In the following activity, you will continue this visualization by thinking about what hospitality you can offer in your classroom.

———————— (Now, complete Activity 1.) ————————

Consider how to offer hospitality in your classroom.

Now, we are going to get more concrete. You are going to look critically at what practices and tone you utilize in your space, and decide whether these are supportive of a hospitable environment or not. This is a safe space to be truthful, even when there is room for growth.

———————— (Complete Activity 2.) ————————

Reflect on the classroom spaces you grew up in.

Now that we've thought about the classroom space we want to develop, we're going to take a step back and think about the classrooms that we experienced growing up. Did they exude similar intentionality and care? Which classrooms did? How did this impact you?

———————— (Now, complete Activity 3.) ————————

ACTIVITIES

1. **Describe the most xenial classroom you can imagine.**

In the space below, visualize being a student walking into a classroom. What would be the most warm, nurturing classroom environment imaginable? What are the things you want to see? Hear? Feel?

_____

_____

_____

_____

2. Consider how to offer hospitality in your classroom.

Make a list below of the things you already do that make the classroom feel hospitable to your students.

_____

_____

_____

Now review the list you made. Are there any areas that can be developed more? Where is there a need that can be filled? Explain what you would hope to add below.

_____

_____

_____

3. Reflect on the classroom spaces you grew up in.

Take a moment to describe the classrooms that you remember below.

_____

_____

_____

A classroom that did not feel welcoming.

_____

_____

_____

A classroom that did feel welcoming.

_____ (Now, complete Reflection 3.) _____

REFLECTIONS

Reflection 1

◉ What did this bring up for you?

◉ How does this shift your thinking around your classroom?

◉ Why does hospitality relate to teaching?

Reflection 2

- How was your mindset about your classroom space before this lesson?

- Has it shifted at all? If so, how?

- Why is making the classroom environment feel more xenial also beneficial to you?

Reflection 3

- What made each classroom feel the way that they did?

- How does reflecting back help you determine the classroom that you strive to have?

- Why should hospitality exist in the classroom?

YOUTUBE, LLC

(A video sharing website that allows members to upload a plethora of short videos.)

Today, children are submerged in a culture of fast moving, entertaining and stunning visual effects. Thus, children are becoming more and more accustomed to viewing high flying special effects; which, in a way, is bad news for teachers. Teachers cannot and must not rely on lecture to provide complete classroom instruction. Teachers in all subject matters should incorporate videos, movie clips and other interactive measures to maximum student's success. Granted, I know making class fun and entertaining isn't in your job description but if you do, most of your behavioral problems will cease and children will enjoy coming to your class.

As a history instructor, I often show clips of films and documentaries to add more realism to my lectures. Movie studios perform extensive research and invest millions of dollars: to recreate significant historical events; to make dated clothes and other minor details that will propel the viewer back into time. Please, use those resources; your students will be attentive guests if they know you are linking your lessons to a film.

Cater to your young audience by feeding their need for special effects by using film clips but that is only half of it; involve them, occasionally pause the film and ask questions to your students. A Chinese proverb suggest, "Tell me and I'll forget; show me and I may remember; involve me and I'll understand."

MENTAL HEALTH LESSON PLAN

Audience: Administrators, Educators, Central Office Personnel & Staff   **Subject:** Mental Health   **Topic:** Youtube, LLC

LESSON GOALS

Reflect on current methods of incorporating technology into the classroom.

- ○ Analyze current student engagement.
- ○ Brainstorm incorporating more interactive activities into your class.

CASEL STANDARDS

- ○ Social Awareness

LESSON OUTLINE

INTRODUCTION

We all have those dreaded memories of being so bored in a class that you are fighting to keep your eyes open. The teacher lectures on and on, and you are not hearing a word of it because all you can think about is what snack you are going to have when you get home from school.

Engaging classrooms are interactive classrooms that draw students in. They are classrooms where the teacher understands when students need to collaborate to feel inspired, need movement to keep up the energy, or need to see a fascinating video to make the learning living to them.

STRATEGIES

Reflect on current methods of incorporating technology into the classroom.

First, we will take a moment to consider what types of technology you incorporate into your classroom. Perhaps there is none, or perhaps there is too much, but wherever you are, take a moment to be candid about that and how this is helping or hurting the engagement of your students.

———————————— *(Now, complete Activity 1.)* ————————————

Analyze current student engagement.

Now you are going to think about the students in your classroom. You will reflect on their level of engagement in class, and you will reflect on their level of engagement when they have a technology break.

———————————— *(Complete Activity 2.)* ————————————

Brainstorm incorporating more interactive activities into your class.

This is the part where you get to get especially creative. Now, in your most ideal classroom, you will think about all of the many ways that you could engage your students. Think out of the box! Don't get bogged down in logistics yet, just let yourself have fun with the possibilities.

———————————— *(Now, complete Activity 3.)* ————————————

ACTIVITIES

1. **Reflect on current methods of incorporating technology into the classroom.**

How do you typically engage your students in learning a new concept?

_____

_____

_____

_____

How is that working?

_____

_____

_____

_____

_____

What are some ways that you could incorporate technology into the lesson to up the engagement of your students?

—————————— (Now, complete Reflection 1.) ——————————

2. **Analyze current student engagement.**

⦿ On an average day, what percent of your students would you say are fully engaged in your lesson?

⦿ What method are you using for engagement?

⦿ Can you think of another method that may be able to improve student engagement?

⊙ How could you incorporate this into your teaching next week?

_____ (Now, complete Reflection 2.) _____

3. **Brainstorm incorporating more interactive activities into your class.**

Below, free write for 4 minutes as many ideas as you can to think of ways to engage your students in the classroom.

_____ (Now, complete Reflection 3.) _____

REFLECTIONS

Reflection 1

⊙ What did you notice in this reflection?

- ⊙ How could incorporating more technology better your students?

- ⊙ How can this be a tool and a resource for you?

Reflection 2

- ⊙ What's it like reflecting on your students' engagement?

- ⊙ What engaged you when you were young?

- ⊙ How can technology broaden access to content for students?

Reflection 3

◉   What did you realize from this activity?

◉   Was there anything you thought of that you're excited to move using forward?

◉   How can you keep this brainstorm somewhere that will motivate and excite you?

ZEAL

(A feeling of strong eagerness; usually in favor of a person or cause.)

What makes your life meaningful? What motivates you to get up every morning? Is it the fact that you have to work to pay bills or is it something deeper? What makes your heart race, pound? Do you find yourself laying awake in the still of the night thinking about the purpose of your life? Do you feel a sense of overwhelming achievement when you reflect on your life? Are you in touch with your life's calling? Do you maximize the benefits of every opportunity? Do you have an eagerness about yourself? Have you gone out your way to support a student? To what cause are you dedicating your life? Are you enjoying every moment of your life? Are you really taking advantage of every second of your life? It is important for teachers to have zeal because it helps them to have a positive attitude towards their job and towards their students. When teachers are passionate about their work, they can go above and beyond to ensure that their students are successful. Zealous teachers are also more likely to stay engaged and motivated in their profession, which can ultimately lead to better outcomes for their students. Additionally, students are more likely to be engaged and motivated themselves when they can see that their teacher is passionate and enthusiastic about teaching. Signs of zeal towards your job are (1) Enthusiasm—Teachers who have zeal for their jobs are enthusiastic about their work of molding young minds. They look forward to the challenge and embrace the hard work associated with reaching the goal; (2) Creativity—Zealous teachers are creative and enjoy finding new and improved ways to overcome challenges and complete the tasks set before them; (3) Willingness to learn—Teachers who have zeal towards their job are always looking for ways to improve their knowledge and skills in order to better serve students; and (4) Positive attitude—Teachers who have zeal are problem solvers, not problem bringers. They have a positive attitude towards their job, their colleagues, and their workplace despite obstacles with which they're faced. Be zealous the work of teaching and you will see that it is contagious!

MENTAL HEALTH LESSON PLAN

Audience: Administrators, Educators, Central Office Personnel & Staff   **Subject:** Mental Health   **Topic:** Zeal

LESSON GOALS

Identify what makes you eager to do the work.

- ○ Reflect on how your teachers got you to invest in learning as a student.
- ○ Consider ways to care for yourself that can support your zeal in the classroom.

CASEL STANDARDS

- ○ Self-Awareness

LESSON OUTLINE

INTRODUCTION

When a teacher is zealous, they are enthusiastic and deeply committed to their work. Their energy is infectious and inspiring to every learner in their space. They go into work every day with their purpose at the forefront of their mind, and even when times get difficult, are able to persevere, knowing that the future of their students is correlated to the intentionality they bring into the classroom each day.

Zealous teachers are willing to go all in. This energy is palpable and can be felt by coworkers, parents, and students. Students are easily convinced that the process of learning is exciting, motivating, and inspiring.

STRATEGIES

Identify what makes you eager to do the work.

In order to feel invested, we have to feel connected to our work. This is why it is important and recommended to connect to your "why" each day before you step foot into the school building. Whether you are working for a better future, working because of your love of content, or working because you want to provide for your family, your rationale matters. It can also be the driving force of your zeal each day.

———————————— *(Now, complete Activity 1.)* ————————————

Reflect on how your teachers helped you invest in learning as a student.

As students, we always remember the teachers who got us to buy into the content they were teaching. Whether this was through an exciting project, an empathetic approach, or an awesome sense of humor, these educators convinced us that the work that we were doing mattered. This intentionality behind engaging your students is mutually beneficial. You see the light in them, which in turn further motivates you.

———————————— *(Complete Activity 2.)* ————————————

Consider ways to care for yourself that can support your zeal in the classroom.

Bringing enthusiasm to the work every day is something easier said than done. The truth is, we can't bring our best selves into the classroom every day unless we commit to our wellbeing first. In this activity, we will consider how you can put on your airplane mask first, so then you can inspire and uplift the young people you serve.

———————————— *(Now, complete Activity 3.)* ————————————

ACTIVITIES

1. **Identify what makes you eager to do the work.**

What is your "why"?

_____

_____

_____

_____

If this is something you don't think about daily, how can you remind yourself of your why each day?

_____

_____

_____

_____

1. **Reflect on how your teachers helped you invest in learning as a student.**

Think of a teacher that really got you to "buy in" to their class, even if it wasn't your favorite. How did they do this? What strategies did they use?

_____

_____

_____

How can you borrow from these strategies to make them feel more authentic to you in the classroom?

_____

_____

_____

(Now, complete Reflection 2.)

1. **Consider ways to care for yourself that can support your zeal in the classroom.**

_____

_____

What fills your cup?

_____

_____

_____

How often are you engaging with these things?

Think of your average week. Where can these things be fit in, so that you are taking care of yourself first?

_____ *(Now, complete Reflection 3.)* _____

REFLECTIONS

Reflection 1

- ⊙ What is your biggest motivator for going to work each day?

- ⊙ How can you keep that at the forefront of your mind?

- ⊙ How does being mindful of your "why" influence your zeal?

Reflection 2

- On a scale of 1-5, how engaging would you rate your class currently?

- How can you use your unique assets to draw students in?

- How can you learn from the educator that initially inspired you?

Reflection 3

- When was the last time you really thought about your self care?

- What are you excited about?

- What will be challenging?

SELECTED PROFESSIONAL EDUCATIONAL ORGANIZATIONS

1. American Alliance for Health, Physical Education, Recreation and Dance
2. American Association of Family & Consumer Sciences
3. American Council on the Teaching of Foreign Language
4. American Library Association
5. American School Counselor Association
6. Association for Career and Technical Education
7. Association for Gifted and Talented Students
8. National Alliance of Black School Educators
9. National Art Education Association
10. National Association for Gifted Children
11. National Association for Music Education
12. National Association of Biology Teachers
13. National Association of Child Care Professionals
14. National Association of Elementary School Principals
15. National Association of Secondary School Principals
16. National Business Education Association
17. National Council for the Social Studies
18. National Council of Teachers of English
19. National Council of Teachers of Mathematics
20. National Rural Education Association
21. National Science Teachers Association
22. Phi Delta Kappa
23. Society for Music Teacher Education

You can perform an internet search on any of the aforementioned professional organizations to obtain additional information such as membership qualifications.

Made in United States
Orlando, FL
22 May 2025